P9-CQM-891

Calm, Alert, and Learning

Classroom Strategies for Self-Regulation

Stuart Shanker

PEARSON

Copyright © 2013 Pearson Canada Inc., Toronto, Ontario.

All rights reserved. This publication is protected by copyright and permission should be obtained from the publisher prior to any prohibited reproduction, storage in a retrieval system, or transmission in any form or by any means, electronic, mechanical, photocopying, recording, or likewise.

Portions of this publication may be reproduced under licence from Access Copyright, or with the express written permission of Pearson Canada Inc., or as permitted by law. Permission to reproduce material from this resource is restricted to the purchasing school.

Permission to reprint copyright material is gratefully acknowledged. Every effort was made to trace ownership of copyright material, secure permission, and accurately acknowledge its use. For information regarding permissions, please contact the Permissions Department through www.pearsoncanada.ca.

The information and activities presented in this work have been carefully edited and reviewed. However, the publisher shall not be liable for any damages resulting, in whole or in part, from the reader's use of this material.

Feedback on this publication can be sent to editorialfeedback@pearsoned.com.

Pearson Canada Inc.
26 Prince Andrew Place
Don Mills, ON M3C 2T8
Customer Service: 1-800-361-6128

5 6 7 8 EBM 16 15 14 13

Publisher: Elynor Kagan
Research and Communications Manager: Mark Cressman
Managing Editor: Joanne Close
Developmental Editors: Anthony Luengo, Anne MacInnes
Assistant Editor: Erin Akerman
Production Editor: Lisa Dimson
Copy Editor: Kathleen ffolliott
Proofreader: Tilman Lewis
Indexer: Jennifer Hedges
Permissions Editor: Christina Beamish
Production Coordinator: Susan Wong
Production Director, School, Print and Digital: Peggy Brown
Cover and Interior Design: David Cheung
Composition: Lapiz Digital Services
Cover Image: ©iStockphoto.com/Ralf Hettler
Manufacturing Coordinator: Karen Bradley
Vice-President, Publishing: Mark Cobham

ISBN: 978-0-13-292713-0

In memory of Stanley Greenspan

©P

Table of Contents

Acknowledgments

This is a book that I had been planning to write with Stanley Greenspan when he was suddenly taken from us. I have laid greater stress on certain areas than Stanley would have done, and no doubt underplayed certain themes that he would have felt deserved greater emphasis. But the resulting book is, I believe, a true representation of the ideas that Stanley spent a lifetime developing and perfecting. These ideas represent a starting point, not a final destination, but what a marvelous starting point Stanley left to us.

It is impossible to thank all the many people who have contributed to this book in one way or another over the years, but certain people clearly stand out whose contribution must be properly acknowledged. Foremost among these are Devin Casenhiser, the Head of Research at MEHRI, and Jim Stieben, the Director of Cognitive and Neuroscience at MEHRI. It is impossible to document all the things I have learned from them over the past seven years about the nature of self-regulation at the behavioural, physiological, and neurobiological levels; about experimental method and analysis; about the madness of doing a randomized control trial; and how the key to our ultimate success was the leadership that they exercised.

The theme that I wish to highlight in the remainder of these acknowledgments is the importance of teamwork in any large undertaking. The most important members of this team for me personally were undoubtedly my current Executive Assistant, Ana Bojcun, and before her, Giselle Tedesco. The demands placed upon them have been unquantifiable, yet both have not only managed to keep MEHRI—and for that matter, me!—running smoothly, but even more remarkable, have remained calm and cheerful in the process.

The team at MEHRI has been a constant source of stimulation and insight. The current team of therapists, collectively known as FACE—Fay McGill, Amanda Binns, Chris Robinson, and Eunice Lee—represent the heart of the research presented in this book. FACE has developed a "Blended Model" to describe their work at MEHRI. Each has trained in the other's clinical area (mental health, speech-language, and occupational therapy), and they share a common office where cases are endlessly discussed, hypotheses formulated, results shared, and hypotheses reformulated.

This interdisciplinary model has informed all of the work that we have done at MEHRI, and it is my pleasure to recognize the invaluable contributions made by Alicia Allison, Lisa Bayrami, Maria Botero, Narmilee Dhayanandhan, Marina Falkovic, Karen Forsyth, Shereen Hassanein, Sonia Khan, Olga Moderer, Jessica Mariano, Sonia Mostrangelo, Nadia Noble, Matt Peterse, and Ljiljana Radenovic. I cannot thank personally here all of the volunteers who have worked at MEHRI over the years, but their contribution has been an absolutely critical factor in our results. We are also grateful to the faculty at the Interdisciplinary Council on Developmental and Learning Disorders (ICDL) who oversaw the DIR training of the MEHRI therapists. A special thanks is owed to Cecilia Breinbauer, Executive Director of ICDL.

How does one properly acknowledge the debt that we owe to the parents and children in our study? We are constantly overwhelmed by their commitment, resilience, and extraordinary spirit. I hope they all realize how many children across Canada will benefit from their efforts.

An essential component of the kind of ambitious research study undertaken at MEHRI is York University. The truth is that none of this would have been possible without the strong support that we received from Rhonda Lenton and Harvey Skinner. I have only a dim awareness of how many times they went to bat for us and I suspect it is just as well that my awareness of this is only dim. My colleagues in the philosophy and psychology departments at York have been no less instrumental, not just by providing me with extensive release-time from teaching so as to focus on this research, but in their constant encouragement and advice.

Friends are an especially important component of the team and so many have helped, but there are four, in particular, I would like to single out: Barbara King, who has been guiding me for more years than either of us would care to remember and has provided important comments on all of the ideas presented here; Roger Downer, who served as Chair for the Board of MEHRI and with whom I have collaborated closely over the past four years; Jane Bertrand, Canada's version of a human Google, who has taught me more about early childhood education than all the books and articles I have read; and Norah Fryer, from whom I have learned so much over the years.

We seldom think to thank our teaching assistants for the work they have done, but in my case it would be unpardonable were I not to express the debt I owe to Jeremy Burman. I would like to say that "together" we have developed a truly exceptional undergraduate course in developmental psychology, but the truth is that he has been the driver and I the passenger in this transformational pedagogical experience.

How do I thank all the teachers I have met across Canada, from whom I have learned so much about teaching and working with children? I have come to recognize that teachers represent the guardians of our future. I wish I knew how to express the gratitude I feel to each and every one of them, both as a parent and as a scientist. There is one person, in particular, I would like to thank in this respect, however, and that is Brenda Whittam-Neary, from whom I have learned so much about introducing self-regulation in the classroom.

I owe a special thanks to my editors at Pearson, Tony Luengo and Joanne Close. Both of them have gone so far above and beyond the call of duty in the preparation of this book that I almost feel self-conscious about listing my name alone as the author. (But note that I said "almost"!) I am also grateful to the reviewers of an earlier draft of this book, Nancy Carl, Pat Dickinson, and Sandy Giles, whose valuable feedback helped guide our work. In addition, I would like to thank Pat for the wonderful section on the cognitive value of play, featured in Chapter 3 (pp. 49–50).

The research on which this book is based was made possible by the extraordinary support of the Milton and Ethel Harris Family Foundation, who provided the funding for the creation of the Milton & Ethel Harris Research Initiative. But my debt to Milt and Ethel Harris goes far beyond this. The vision on which MEHRI is based—the idea of studying the nature of self-regulation and techniques for enhancing it—was entirely Milt's, and then carefully nurtured by Ethel following Milt's tragic early death, and thanks to the tremendous individual support of David, Judith, Naomi, and John Harris.

I am also grateful for the support we have received from the Unicorn Foundation, Cure Autism Now, the Public Health Agency of Canada, the Templeton Foundation, and York University.

Words do not suffice to thank my parents and sister, but at least they mark a start.

Finally, I want to thank my wife and children. They are the true inspiration for this book: the foundation for everything I do and everything I want to do.

Introduction

We are in the midst of a revolution in educational thinking and practice. Scientific advances in a number of fields point to a similar argument—that how well students do in school can be determined by how well they are able to self-regulate. Some theorists believe that self-regulation should now be considered a more important indicator of educational performance than IQ (Blair & Diamond, 2008; Duckworth & Seligman, 2005; Shonkoff & Phillips, 2000).

So what is self-regulation and what does it look like in your classroom?

Educational research in the area of self-regulation has been largely concerned with such matters as a student's ability to set goals and monitor progress; seek clarification or assistance when needed; assess and reflect critically on personal learning strengths and weaknesses; and employ learning strategies and aids to assist in problem solving (Zimmerman, 1994). These traits are especially relevant to the adolescent learner. Indeed, the neural systems related to these functions are amongst the last to mature in the growth of the human brain. But over the past decade our understanding of the development of self-regulation in the early years, which lays the foundation for these higher metacognitive functions, has moved forward in a number of domains.

©P

One of the best sources of research on these foundational aspects of self-regulation is Roy Baumeister and Kathleen Vohs's *Handbook of Self-Regulation: Research, Theory, and Applications* (2011). In the handbook, the various authors involved describe self-regulation as the ability to

1. attain, maintain, and change one's level of energy to match the demands of a task or situation

2. monitor, evaluate, and modify one's emotions

3. sustain and shift one's attention when necessary and ignore distractions

4. understand both the meaning of a variety of social interactions and how to engage in them in a sustained way

5. connect with and care about what others are thinking and feeling—to empathize and act accordingly

When we think of students who are successful in our classrooms, we see evidence of these abilities. When we think of students who are less successful, we can just as easily see evidence that one or more of these abilities needs strengthening. Perhaps a student cannot break her attention on a task to start to listen to her teacher. Another student may be desperate to have friends but constantly misses the social cues his peers provide. Both students exhibit difficulties in domains of self-regulation.

Self-regulation is increasingly being seen as essential for enabling children to respond efficiently and effectively to the everyday challenges they face in and out of school. The better we understand self-regulation, the better we can implement educational strategies that enhance students' capacity to learn and develop the skills necessary to deal with life's challenges. Many of us are at the beginning of this journey and no doubt will learn much more about self-regulation and how we can enhance it in every child in every classroom. For now, I hope this resource will provide a foundation for understanding what self-regulation is, what it looks like, and how to foster it in your classroom.

©P

The Five-Domain Model of Self-Regulation

In this resource, we look at self-regulation through an exploration of five domains:

1. The Biological Domain

2. The Emotional Domain

3. The Cognitive Domain

4. The Social Domain

5. The Prosocial Domain

In each of us, there are complex links between and among these five domains. We will explore those links more deeply in the chapters that follow. To get started, we will outline each domain. Keep in mind that, throughout this introduction and the following chapters, our primary goal is to help students to achieve *optimal self-regulation*, a state of calm focus and alertness appropriate for learning in a classroom.

There are six critical elements to optimal self-regulation. These elements span the five domains and represent, in a concise way, what we hope we can help you to move toward with your students.

Six Critical Elements to Optimal Self-Regulation

- when feeling calmly focused and alert, the ability to know that one is calm and alert

- when one is stressed, the ability to recognize what is causing that stress

- the ability to recognize stressors both within and outside the classroom

- the desire to deal with those stressors

- the ability to develop strategies for dealing with those stressors

- the ability to recover efficiently and effectively from dealing with stressors

The Domains: An Overview

The Biological Domain

The biological domain of self-regulation refers to activity, or the level of energy, in the human nervous system. Levels of energy can and do vary widely from person to person and from situation to situation. Such levels vary depending on an individual's temperament and the situation he or she is in. The following are some common examples of how children can vary in their levels of energy and, as a result, how they respond to their environment.

Some children

- are extremely sensitive (hypersensitive) to a form of sensory input in their environment, whether it be auditory, visual, tactile (touch), olfactory (smell), or gustatory (taste). For example, a child who is hypersensitive to sound may be negatively affected by noise made by other children in the playground or by the sounds of bells or buzzers used to control classroom transitions. In this case, the child may try to minimize the noise physically by covering her ears or psychologically by disengaging from her environment.

- have difficulty sitting still for longer than a few minutes. These children need to move around the classroom and to change their position multiple times in an hour. For some of these children, even sitting on a hard chair taxes their nervous system—they become fidgety and will move to lessen the unpleasant sensations they experience when sitting.

- have a nervous system that quickly becomes overloaded with multiple forms of what for most people would be considered normal sensory input

In the case of the last example, these children have two common responses to overload:

1. Shut out the stimuli. These children become withdrawn (hypoalert). In this state, while their nervous system is no longer

on overload, they are not aroused sufficiently to be able to learn. These children need to learn how to *up*-regulate (increase their level and expenditure of energy).

2. Become overstimulated. These children become hyperalert and need to learn how to *down*-regulate (decrease their level and expenditure of energy).

Now, take a look around your classroom. You will no doubt see at least one child who is doodling, twiddling a pencil, lightly drumming fingers on a desk, jiggling feet, or stretching. Another child may be flitting from one activity to another. In both cases these children might unconsciously engage in such behaviours to try to remain or become calmly focused and alert. In other words, these children are self-regulating their nervous system to allow for optimal functioning.

The big question for teachers is this: *What are the regulating techniques that can be used to help children who either need to up-regulate (become more alert) or down-regulate (become more calm) so that they can pay close attention to instructions and to the contributions of other students without disrupting the flow of the class?* You will find some of these techniques as they particularly apply to the biological domain in Chapter 1 (pp. 1–21).

The Emotional Domain

Children's behaviour in the emotional domain—the realm of feelings and moods—is generally easy to identify. This is particularly so, of course, in the case of strong emotions, both positive and negative. Some common examples include

- becoming overly excited when receiving praise for an assignment

- exhibiting intense frustration at being unable to solve a problem

- becoming paralyzed with fear on spotting a well-known bully in the schoolyard

Here is what we know intuitively and what we experience as adults: positive emotions, such as interest, curiosity, and happiness, generate energy. Negative emotions, on the other hand, consume energy. Think back on your day. What events or interactions picked you up? What events made you feel tired and unfocused? Our students are no different.

This makes the emotional domain a very challenging area of self-regulation. Intense negative emotions—anger, fear, frustration, sadness, and anxiety, as examples—can make it very difficult for some students to establish and maintain a state of optimal self-regulation. Without this regulation, it is difficult for these students to pay attention.

Picture this situation: a Kindergarten teacher is reading a story to a group of children. She poses a question to the group and selects a student to share her answer. Another student has his hand up and is very eager to share his thoughts. Impatient and now angry because the teacher did not select him, the student blurts out his answer. The teacher, recognizing the child's impatience, gently explains that he has to wait his turn. Her response helps the child to calm down, or down-regulate. Techniques for helping students to improve their emotional regulation are included in Chapter 2 (pp. 22–44).

The Cognitive Domain

The cognitive domain relates to mental processes such as memory, attention, the acquisition and retention of information, and problem solving. As a teacher, you will no doubt find this area of self-regulation the most familiar. Optimal self-regulation in this domain means that a student can efficiently sustain and switch attention, sequence his or her thoughts, keep several pieces of information in his or her mind at the same time, ignore distractions, and inhibit impulsive behaviour. As you will see in Chapter 3 (pp. 45–72), certain practices have proved to be very effective in helping children develop these skills, especially once they have become more adept at self-regulation in the biological and emotional domains.

The Social Domain

Children vary considerably in their capacity for self-regulation in the social domain. A student who is optimally regulated in this domain understands, assesses, and acts on particular social cues and in general

    ©P

behaves in a socially appropriate manner. Students who struggle in this domain have much more difficulty understanding cues. For example, a student may misinterpret an invitation to express an opinion as an opportunity to dominate or continually interrupt a group discussion. Another student may become withdrawn because he misinterprets a teacher's offer to help him with an assignment as a sign that the teacher thinks he is not smart enough to do it on his own.

Now commonly referred to as *social intelligence*, this capacity to understand social situations and function optimally in them begins from infancy. It develops as children gradually internalize—initially from their caregivers and later from their peers and teachers—the meaning of subtle social cues such as facial expressions and tones of voice. Understanding these cues is especially important for developing a child's ability to play cooperatively with other children and successfully interact in groups within and outside of the classroom (Greenspan & Shanker, 2004). Misunderstanding a social situation, one child may push too hard when dealing with others, while another may not push hard enough. If a child is experiencing problems in the social domain, this can profoundly affect his or her biological and emotional self-regulation and vice versa. You will find some helpful techniques for dealing with such situations in the social domain in Chapter 4 (pp. 73–92).

The Prosocial Domain

Psychologists have traditionally thought of the prosocial domain as autonomous, as simply the realm in which individuals engage in behaviours that are positive and helpful and that promote social acceptance, friendship, and—very critically—empathy (Eisenberg & Mussen, 1989). Over the past decade, however, we have learned that a child's prosocial functioning is intimately bound up with all of the other areas in our five-domain model of self-regulation (Eisenberg, Smith, & Spinrad, 2011).

Take a child who sees that his friend is crying, perhaps because she has just hurt herself while playing in the schoolyard. If he is optimally self-regulated in the different domains, the boy will

- pay attention to what has happened (cognitive domain)

- remain calm in the situation (biological and emotional domains)

- understand what his friend is feeling (social domain)

- do something to help alleviate the friend's distress (prosocial domain)

However, what if this boy finds this situation very difficult to deal with because he is very withdrawn? In that case, he may easily become **dysregulated** in all five domains. For a start, he might

Dysregulation—an impairment or interruption of a regulatory system that interferes with a child's ability to regulate him- or herself in a domain

- not pay sufficient attention to understand exactly what has happened (cognitive domain)

- find himself overwhelmed by the manifestations of his friend's feelings (e.g., her loud crying) and become upset himself (biological and emotional domains)

- be unable to process how his friend is feeling about the situation because he is too stressed (social domain)

- be unable to help his friend in any way (prosocial domain)

Here is a similar situation and one that is instructive for illustrating not only how the domains interact with one another, but also how the teacher involved responded to encourage self-regulation, notably in the prosocial domain.

Two six-year-olds were playing at recess when one fell. The girl reacted to her friend's fall and subsequent distress by laughing and hitting him on the back. This, of course, upset her friend even further, leading the girl, in turn, to laugh even more and hit the boy again as she became more hyperaroused. The teacher on duty, knowing that the girl had great difficulty with social conventions and controlling her motor actions when hyperaroused, intervened as follows: She showed the girl how to console her friend by softly telling him that everything would be all right. She then demonstrated for the child how to pat her friend *gently* on the back. Almost instantly, both children down-regulated.

If we look at this situation and apply how we might instinctively act, we see that there is potential for the teacher to admonish the girl for being too rough. In this instance, chances are that the girl (and her friend) would have become even more upset and dysregulated. As it was, the girl genuinely wanted to be kind, but her poor social skills and problems with motor control made this difficult. With the wrong

©P

kind of adult response, the girl might continue to have ongoing problems in the prosocial domain. With her teacher's keen understanding and gentle encouragement, however, the girl was able to learn an appropriate response to the situation and model it. With similar interventions, this girl can learn the social skills necessary to foster and enjoy close friendships, in turn paving the way for the development of prosocial skills. This teacher was much like Rose, another educator with a keen understanding of the importance of the prosocial domain. You will learn about this teacher's classroom practices in Chapter 5 (pp. 93–119).

Contributing Forces: MEHRI and the Work of Stanley Greenspan

In this resource, you will see references to the Milton & Ethel Harris Research Initiative (MEHRI). I have been involved with this program for a number of years and before that with Stanley Greenspan, the developer of the Floortime™ technique to support healthy child development. What follows is a brief overview of the goals and achievements of both MEHRI and Stanley Greenspan.

In 2005, MEHRI was established at York University, with a significant grant from the Harris Steel Foundation. This was complemented with generous support from The Harris Family Foundation, York University, and grants from several other sources—among them Cure Autism Now (merged with Autism Speaks in 2007), the Public Health Agency of Canada, the Templeton Foundation, and the Unicorn Children's Foundation.

MEHRI was created to pursue two mandates. The first was to study the efficacy of MEHRIT (the Milton & Ethel Harris Research Initiative Treatment program), a relational intervention for young children with autism based on the Developmental Individual Difference Relationship-based (DIR®) model developed by Stanley Greenspan and Serena Wieder. The preliminary goal of MEHRIT is to both help parents in their efforts to regulate their child and to teach the child how to self-regulate. This therapy, and the results that have been obtained, will be described in Chapter 6 (pp. 120–133).

Developmental Individual Difference Relationship-based (DIR®) Model

The second mandate of MEHRI is to build a universal model of self-regulation, one that would benefit *all* children. I had the great fortune to serve as the first President of Fraser Mustard's Council for Early Child Development. Mustard trained me in the complexities involved in scaling up any such initiative, and introduced me to many civil service officials, superintendents, and principals in Canada and internationally who made it possible for MEHRI to work with teachers and schools, and to pilot the techniques that are described in this resource.

Canadian Self-Regulation Initiative

Since the first printing of this book, the MEHRI team has begun working with a number of educators in British Columbia and Ontario on the Canadian Self-Regulation Initiative, under the leadership of Mike McKay, Superintendent and CEO of the Surrey School District. This is truly a grassroots phenomenon. It grew from the work of Dave Hutchinson, the Superintendent of the Nanaimo School District, who began piloting these ideas in Saskatchewan. More and more teachers and administrators began asking if we could help them institute similar self-regulation practices in their classes and schools. What has evolved from these discussions is the First Wave, which involves six school districts in BC and two in Ontario and a number of associate members in both provinces. This project promises to transform the practice of early and secondary education.

As you read the chapters that follow, you will encounter "Applications in the Classroom" sections that help to situate self-regulation in school settings. It is important to note that the roots of these applications stemmed from contact with MEHRI. In addition, some of these applications are composites, including material from other MEHRI initiatives.

Self-Regulation in the 21st Century

There has been an explosion of research on self-regulation over the past decade in a range of domains:

- developmental disorders (Greenspan, Wieder, & Simons, 1998; Lillas & Turnbull, 2009)
- internalizing problems (Lewis & Todd, 2007)

©P

- externalizing problems (Ross & Fontao, 2008; Stieben et al., 2007)

- personality disorders (Bradley, 2000)

- memory disorders (Gunnar & Quevedo, 2007)

- alcoholism and risky behaviours (Crockett, Raffaelli, & Shen, 2006)

- obesity (Riggs, Sakuma, & Pentz, 2007)

- diabetes and cancer (Grossarth-Maticek & Eysenck, 1995)

- coronary heart disease (Boersma & Maes, 2006)

- immune system disorders, including asthma, allergies, chronic fatigue syndrome, and rheumatoid arthritis (McEwen, 2002)

To be sure, each of these problems is thought to have a unique biological basis and/or contributing environmental factors, and thus to follow a different developmental pathway. And within each disorder there is thought to be enormous variability in the pathways. But the biological challenges in each are thought to be made worse by problems in self-regulation, starting early in the child's development, and contributing to significant **downstream** effects.

The better we understand the complex biological and experiential interactions involved in self-regulation, the better we can design classroom practices that will enhance a student's self-regulation and mitigate the cascading effects of initial challenges. So compelling is this vision that one might go so far as to argue that if IQ was the major psychological construct of the 20th century, in the 21st century it will be self-regulation; for unlike IQ, this new lens gives us the hope that by providing children with tools to promote their self-regulation, we can significantly alter their educational—and life—trajectories.

Downstream— happening at a later stage

What Is Self-Regulation?

About This Book and Website

As you read, you will notice icons in page margins. These icons, one to denote research and the other to denote parent material, alert you to resources found on the book's companion website: www.pearsoncanada.ca/cal. Here you will find resources, including articles, links to research and related sites, and parent materials, organized by chapter and topic.

©P

Chapter 1

The Biological Domain

Key Attributes of the Biological Domain

Children who are optimally self-regulated in the biological domain will demonstrate these key attributes:

- physical health, which includes a robust immune system

- sufficient energy on waking up, which is maintained through the course of the day

- the ability to recoup energy after difficult experiences

- the ability to remain calm amid distracting visual and auditory stimuli

- the ability to follow healthy daily routines (e.g., healthy diet, sufficient exercise, required hours of sleep)

- engagement in—and enjoyment of—physical activities, enabled by well-functioning motor systems that, for example, allow the coordination of arms and legs and of eyes and fingers

The physical mechanisms of self-regulation are found in the human nervous system, which is part of the biological domain. As teachers, we need to think about this domain when we deal with issues of self-regulation in the other four domains (emotional, cognitive, social, and prosocial). Know that if a student has self-regulation issues in the biological domain, it is extremely likely that he or she will have issues in at least one other domain. Furthermore, challenges in the other domains can exacerbate problems in the biological domain.

Autonomic Nervous System—the system that controls many organs and muscles within our body. It is divided into two parts: the sympathetic nervous system and parasympathetic nervous system.

Sympathetic Nervous System (SNS)—the system for acceleration that results in quick action

Parasympathetic Nervous System (PNS, occasionally PSNS)—the system for recovery or slowing down to a condition of rest. PNS can refer to the peripheral nervous system (the nerves and ganglia outside of the brain and spinal cord) and the parasympathetic nervous system. An online search for PNS usually results in the former.

Adrenaline—the hormone involved in acceleration

The Human Nervous System and Self-Regulation

To begin, we need a basic understanding of two major elements of the nervous system that affect our biological self-regulation: the **sympathetic nervous system (SNS)** and the **parasympathetic nervous system (PNS)**. Both are part of the **autonomic nervous system**, which controls many organs and muscles within our body—in most cases without our being aware of it.

The nature and basic functions—and malfunctions—of the SNS and PNS are summarized in Figure 1.1.

Figure 1.1: Overview of the Sympathetic and Parasympathetic Nervous Systems

Sympathetic Nervous System (SNS)

- This system is for acceleration that results in quick action. The hormone **adrenaline** is involved in this acceleration. For example, a shy student is asked to read in front of her class. Her body releases adrenaline in response to the stress her body experiences (increased heart rate and rapid breathing).
- Overacceleration or prolonged activation of this system results in hyperalertness and a rapid depletion of energy.
- When the SNS is excessively engaged, it can result in a hypersensitive response of fight, flight, or freeze that is triggered in inappropriate situations, in some ways like a car alarm that goes off when a leaf brushes against the hood of a car. In this instance, a child's stress response might be out of all proportion to the event that triggered it.

©P

Parasympathetic Nervous System (PNS)

- This system is for recovery or slowing down to a condition of rest. The hormone **cortisol** is involved in this recovery process.

- Too much or prolonged de-acceleration of this system can result in hypoactive states such as prolonged lethargy or withdrawal—the child who watches television indiscriminately, who "zones out," or who daydreams excessively are examples.

- Excessive activation of the SNS, which in turn demands excessive activation of the PNS, can result in a reduced ability to recover from fight, flight, or freeze situations.

Cortisol—the hormone involved in slowing down to a condition of rest

In simple terms, when the SNS and the PNS are in a balanced state (homeostasis), they can be "turned on and turned off again efficiently and not too frequently" (McEwen, 2006, p. 33). An analogy is your home heating system. You set your thermostat to 21°—your homeostatic point. It is cool outside, so the temperature in your house begins to dip below your desired temperature. To compensate, your furnace turns on. In this example, the furnace turning on can be compared to a person's SNS being activated by stress. Your furnace runs until the temperature reaches 21° again. Then it shuts off—the shutting down can be compared to your PNS being activated to compensate for the activation of your SNS. Now imagine that your thermostat does not work properly. Your furnace runs constantly trying to reach its goal of 21°. This can be compared to a person's overworked, overstressed SNS system. To compensate, the PNS must overwork to achieve a balanced state.

As Figure 1.2 shows, there is a continuum of energy, and the amount of down-regulating (PNS) or up-regulating (SNS) necessary to achieve an optimal state for learning—the point at which a child is calmly focused and alert—varies from child to child and from situation to situation.

Figure 1.2: Continuum of Energy in the Human Nervous System

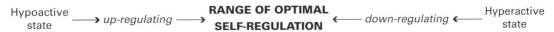

Hypoactive state → up-regulating → **RANGE OF OPTIMAL SELF-REGULATION** ← down-regulating ← Hyperactive state

Note: The most hypoactive state is sleep; the most hyperactive state is a tantrum.

A driving analogy can help us to understand the subtle energy adjustments involved in regulating attention according to the demands of an activity. Think of driving in rush-hour traffic. A novice driver may tend to push too hard on the gas pedal or suddenly slam on the brakes, causing the car to lurch forward or screech to a stop. An experienced driver can modulate the gas and brake pedals efficiently, smoothly, and effortlessly, but an inexperienced driver needs practice to learn how to do this. The same is true for maintaining optimal self-regulation, especially in social situations, and especially for children. Children need practice in learning how to adjust to variances in activity levels (for example, up-regulating for a math quiz or down-regulating after recess) so that they can achieve—and maintain—a calm, alert state.

Self-regulation in the biological domain can best be understood in terms of the countervailing [counteracting] forces of SNS activation and PNS de-acceleration. This involves, in effect, putting your foot on the gas or on the brakes in order to deal with a stressor and then recover.

Maintaining Optimal Self-Regulation in the Classroom

When we talk about a child's ability to achieve optimal self-regulation, we refer to the child's ability to make changes to his or her arousal level quickly and easily so that it matches the energy needed to deal calmly and efficiently with the task at hand (Gonzalez-Lima & Scheich, 1985; Lillas & Turnbull, 2009).

> Alert processing sustains smooth functioning within the body, awareness of internal and external stimuli, attention to relevant information, a capacity for abrupt shifts or gradual changes of energy and emotion, and the capacity for interpersonal engagement with expressions of joy. This state is the hallmark of awake regulation because it provides the optimal baseline for learning. (Lillas & Turnbull, 2009, p. 142)

As you know, children vary considerably in their ability to self-regulate in the social interactions of learning. To return to our driving analogy, one child may constantly push too hard on the accelerator (the overly excited child who cannot wait for instructions before beginning a task, for example), while another presses too hard on the brakes (the withdrawn child who does not interact with his peers

                                                                 ©P

unless asked). Yet another child might jump erratically back and forth between accelerating and de-accelerating in her behaviour.

The more hypoaroused a child is, the less inclined he or she will be to *become* engaged in the social interactions of learning. The more hyperaroused the child is, the less able he or she will be to *remain* engaged in such interactions. For example, a hypoaroused child who is overly absorbed by an object, studying it intensely or playing with it, is likely to miss out on guidance from the teacher and on shared learning experiences with other children. Similarly, a hyperaroused child who darts around the room—constantly changing his focus of attention from one object or activity to the next—cannot sustain the necessary focus to learn. In what follows, we will look at simple techniques for up-regulating the first kind of child and down-regulating the second.

While it may seem that a child simply has to match energy levels to the varying learning situations in a classroom, optimal self-regulation is more than that. It also requires a child to match his or her energy levels to meet the demands of a situation in a *maximally efficient manner*. For example, the less energy required on a child's part to engage in social interaction, the longer the child will be able to sustain that interaction. As a result, there will be a greater opportunity for learning to occur (Tomkins, 1963).

This concept—a maximally efficient manner—is key. Take the child who is engaged in an exciting soccer game during gym class. The child's next class is math. She quickly and easily down-regulates her energy level—from the energy needed for the high-octane game to a calm, alert focus required for math. Now picture another student, in the same gym class and the same math activity. He is still caught up in the excitement of the soccer game and has trouble down-regulating to the point that he can focus on the math lesson. It is harder for him to match his arousal level to the task—it takes longer and it takes more of his energy. This leaves him with less energy to attend to his learning.

Interpreting a Child's Behaviour

As a teacher, you know that interpreting children's behaviour is not always straightforward. A child who is chronically hypoaroused, for

"It is quite within the realm of possibility that we may be able to iron out the peaks and valleys of energy utilization for a more sustained but less intensive positive affective experience, or exaggerate them for a more intense experience of alertness, high energy, and positive affect...."
— **Tomkins, 1963, p. 21**

example, might be in a withdrawn state for one or more of the following reasons:

- difficulty reaching a threshold to activate awareness of a stimulus (e.g., for some reason the child does not hear and respond to a teacher calling her name)

- withdraws as a defence mechanism because certain stimuli or experiences are overwhelming (e.g., too much noise or loud talking)

- difficulty differentiating internal signals (e.g., does not realize when his body is telling him that he is hungry or cold)

- difficulty integrating sensations of touch with the information coming from limbs, joints, and deep muscles (e.g., has trouble sitting down in a chair without arms, or is constantly bumping into furniture or other children)

- difficulty coordinating sensations with motor responses and sequencing actions (e.g., looks around in all directions when the teacher calls her name because she has trouble locating the source of the sound)

For one or more of these reasons, a child might find it very soothing to remain in a hypoaroused state for a prolonged period of time. This child may show that he is hypoaroused by his lack of engagement in a learning task, as one example, or by prolonged periods of daydreaming as another example.

Similarly, there are various reasons to explain the behaviour of chronically hyperaroused children, the most common of which are

- hypersensitivity (overly sensitive) to certain kinds of internal or external stimuli (e.g., certain noises or colours)

- too many stressors for that child (e.g., overcrowding)

- sensory craving—a need to get more of a stimulus, such as a sound or tactile sensation, to register that stimulus (e.g., a child humming fulfills her need for an auditory stimulus, while a child who sucks his lip or chews a pencil is fulfilling the need for an oral stimulus)

- a need to maintain a certain level of activity in order to feel fully aware of his or her body or to remain calm in a certain environment (e.g., a child who, when seated, constantly moves his feet)

Correctly interpreting a child's behaviour also means recognizing that the same or similar behaviours in two children can reflect different states in each of them, as well as different attempts at self-regulation. Some children's attempts are more successful than others. Consider, for example, the following three scenarios.

How Biological States Affect Children's Behaviour

Scenario 1: Sleeping and Waking Up

Child A has a good night's sleep, a critical way of restoring the state of equilibrium that underpins optimal self-regulation. He jumps out of bed in the morning in a burst of energy, feeling revitalized, calm, and ready to face the world—and to pay attention at school.

Child B does not sleep enough. She wakes up in a hyperactive state that reflects great expenditure of energy as she tries to achieve equilibrium. This state of "overdrive" further tires her out so that she is not alert enough to face the challenges of the school day.

Bedtime Routines

Scenario 2: Daydreaming

Child C very briefly daydreams during an activity, doing so to quickly restore a state of calm that allows her to pay attention.

Child D daydreams for prolonged periods, which results in his becoming hypoalert and therefore unable to pay sufficient attention in class.

Scenario 3: Sitting Still in a Classroom

Child E is comfortable sitting still in his chair because it helps him to focus his attention during a discussion.

Child F tries to sit still in her chair but is uncomfortable doing so, which makes her fidgety and unable to focus on anything but her discomfort.

These scenarios show how the same or similar behaviour in different children can indicate either optimal self-regulation or a lack of it.

It is also important to note the following:

1. There is a very close connection between calmness, alertness, and learning. To say that a child is attentive is to say that he or she is neither hypo- nor hyperaroused. A child is best ready to learn when she is calm and alert.

2. Being focused and alert can be as much a matter of up-regulation as down-regulation, as much a matter of experiencing the positive feelings that fuel sustained attention as modulating the negative ones that drain it. Child A, for example, is up-regulating as he jumps out of bed, while Child C is down-regulating, recovering, when she daydreams for a moment. Note, too, that each of them does so quickly, a reflection of the maximal efficiency noted earlier as a requirement of optimal regulation.

3. Some children have to use more energy than others to achieve a state of equilibrium, resulting in a vicious cycle: the more energy they consume, the less able they are to self-regulate efficiently, and subsequently the less energy they have to attend. For example, the amount of energy being consumed by Child B is debilitating, while the brief burst of energy seen in Child A is invigorating.

As we shall begin to explore in the latter part of this chapter, a number of self-regulation techniques that teachers can implement in the classroom are proving to be highly effective at helping students to achieve optimal regulation. These techniques are simple and easy to implement, and when practised consistently and patiently, can be of enormous benefit to the student.

Research on the Development of Self-Regulation in Infants

Before we move on to the second section of this chapter, let us consider three important findings from research on the development of self-regulation in infants and very young children.

©P

Children acquire the ability to self-regulate by first being regulated.
Picture a mother or other caregiver trying to soothe a screaming infant. The child is clearly hyperaroused. As a newborn, the child has a few innate regulating mechanisms (such as falling asleep) but no capacity to deliberately self-regulate. It is up to the adult, then, to regulate the child using a variety of techniques, such as soothing facial expressions, gestures, and vocalizations. In effect, a sort of "wireless" connection (Tantam, 2009) for regulation is established that lays the foundation for self-regulation. In time, as the child's capacity to pay attention to her caregiver increases, she internalizes the regulating intention of these techniques, thereby developing her own capacity for self-regulation (Greenspan & Shanker, 2004; Legerstee, 2005; McCain, Mustard, & Shanker, 2007).

Some children have difficulty internalizing these techniques. As a result, they will continue to require a fair amount of external regulation well into their school years to help them become better at self-regulating. You may also find that a student needs help in self-regulating in one situation but not in another. For example, a student may become hyperaroused by particular sounds but remain calm around most visual stimuli.

It is also important to recognize that the more hypo- or hyper-aroused a child is, the more difficulty that child will have reading his or her own internal body cues—those that tell the child when he or she is tired or hungry, hot or cold, or, even, when he or she might be hurt. One teacher taught a very excitable boy who always came to class in a T-shirt no matter what the weather was like. One day she noticed that the boy was shivering and had goosebumps all over his arms, yet he had not put on the sweater that his mother had put in his backpack. That was when the teacher realized that the boy did not know he was cold. Over the next few months, the teacher put in place some of the regulating practices outlined in this chapter. The "magical moment" occurred when the boy came to her and asked her if she could fetch him a blanket and help him settle in a large beanbag chair for a rest.

Adults around children need to be optimally regulated themselves.
Adults around children—parents, caregivers, and teachers—face great demands on their own energy resources, which can make it difficult for them to remain optimally regulated. Arousal levels can be

"The interbrain, I will argue, is composed of brains (obviously, but it is important to note that I am not describing the kinds of connection that might occur between minds) linked by the wireless communication of intentions and not information."
— Tantam, 2009, p. 17

"In the explosive development that takes place between nine and eighteen months, a baby… learns to regulate her moods and behaviour and perceive and organize patterns to form a more complete sense of self."
— Greenspan & Shanker, 2004, p. 60

Interactive Regulation

"In the definition of interactive regula-tion, we use the terms 'mutual,' 'bi-directional' and 'co-constructed' regulation interchange-ably. These terms do not imply 'mutuality'; instead, they refer to the contribution that each partner makes to the regulation of the exchange."

— **Beebe & Lachmann, 1998, p. 4**

The Importance of Parental Self-Regulation

contagious: think of how someone's energy-depleting anger can trig-ger an angry, energy-depleting response in the person to whom the anger is directed. Similarly, a caregiver around a chronically hyper- or hypoaroused child has to work very hard to regulate that child, which can be quite draining for the caregiver. The better the caregiver can stay calmly focused and alert herself, maintaining or quickly restor-ing her own equilibrium, the better she can help the child to establish and sustain a similar optimal state (Beebe & Lachmann, 1998). And, as we know, talking softly and slowly to calm an upset child can help to calm the caregiver down as well.

It immediately follows from this last point that a central con-cern of this resource, which we will look at more closely in the final chapter, is our own self-regulation as educators. Clearly, the better *we* can remain optimally regulated, the better we can help a student to achieve optimal regulation. But even more important is that the bet-ter we regulate ourselves, the more energized we feel at the end of the teaching day and the more refreshed we feel the next morning.

Regulating a child involves modulating the intensity of stimuli in order to engage and sustain the child's attention.

Research on infants shows that a critical aspect of regulating involves modulating the intensity of a stimulus so that a baby's attention is engaged and sustained. Some babies love a colourful mobile over their crib; some are overwhelmed by it. By experimenting with different types of touch, tones of voice, facial expressions, postures, gestures, and so on, caregivers discover which types of adult behaviours best suit a baby's temperament. They learn which behaviours capture the child's attention and help him or her to relax and avoid slipping into a hypo- or hyperaroused state.

> Some babies are very sensitive and require gentle soothing. Some are underreactive and require more energetic wooing. Some babies begin to figure out patterns of sights or sounds quickly; some slowly. Some readily turn toward sound or sights, but others take a while to notice. These responses happen more readily if adults tailor their approaches to each infant based on her individual preferences and abilities. (Greenspan & Shanker, 2004, p. 55)

©P

Much the same holds true for older children in classrooms. As a teacher, you may speak quietly to one child, reduce noise stimuli for another, and seat a third child in an area with less visual stimuli. These are all ways in which you can encourage and support self-regulation in your students. Practical details on that and more follow in the next section.

How Parenting Supports Biological Self-Regulation

Applications in the Classroom

Scenario

Doris has been a Grade 1 teacher for 10 years. She loves her job and her students love her. In the last few years, however, she has started to find her work much more draining. It is not that she is losing her commitment, but the students themselves seem to be changing. When Doris started teaching, her class contained a few challenging students who needed additional attention. Now, even within this short time span, it seems as if half of her class is composed of children who cannot sit still or respond to their name, much less listen to a story.

Doris approached MEHRI for help in dealing with this situation. She sought advice that would help her students, restore her enthusiasm to get started each morning, and give her a sense of satisfaction for a job well done at the end of the day.

Classroom Makeover

The first area of focus was the physical set-up of Doris's classroom. Doris was so accustomed to her classroom's visual stimuli (posters, wall calendars, pictures, and mobiles) that she barely noticed them. But perhaps the same was not the case for her students. When it was observed that there was not a paper out of place on Doris's own desk, she was asked to describe her home office. As anticipated, Doris stated that she could not stand clutter, and the tidier her office, the more productively she worked. Was the same true for the children in her class? If some of her students were part of the increasing number

©P

of children who are easily overwhelmed by visual or auditory stimuli, an effective first step would be to reduce this overload through a "classroom makeover."

Visual Environment

For a number of years, educational programs such as Reggio Emilia have asserted that children concentrate better in a classroom with a reduced number of visual distractors. Ideal environments have lots of natural light, a minimum of artificial light, and walls painted in subdued pastels with a non-gloss finish rather than vibrant colours. To reduce visual overload, Doris began to tackle her classroom set-up from top to bottom.

Inspired by the Reggio Emilia philosophy, Doris undertook the first part of her classroom makeover. She stripped off the more dizzying wall ornaments, and reduced the amount of material on her bulletin and whiteboards. After making a quick trip to purchase wicker baskets and labels, Doris proceeded to put everyday classroom materials in labelled baskets, and other supplies away in cupboards. In taking these steps, she hoped to reduce the distraction of visual clutter for the children.

Interestingly, after this first step in her classroom makeover, Doris remarked that *she* felt calmer when she walked into the room. This is important, for self-regulation is as much about the teacher's state as that of his or her students (see pp. 9–10 on the importance of self-regulation for teachers). If Doris feels calm, her students will be more likely to feel calm. And the calmer Doris feels, the better she will be able to deal with her challenging students.

Auditory Environment

While changing the general appearance of the room was an important first step, research on self-regulation has now firmly established that auditory stimuli are by far the most powerful of all distractors (Bendixen et al., 2010). This made sense to Doris, who noticed how upset her challenging students became when they heard the school buzzer that signalled transitions. Her principal agreed to institute a chime in place of a buzzer to signify transitions, but a problem remained: How could Doris manage in-class transitions?

The Reggio Emilia Approach

"The educators of Reggio Emilia view the school as a living organism. A place of shared relationships among the children, the teachers, and the parents. The school produces for the adults, but above all for the children, a feeling of belonging in a world that is alive, welcoming, and authentic."

— Malaguzzi, n.d., para. 13

©P

Occupational therapists suggested using sounds made by drums, Tibetan gongs, singing bowls, and even music. Doris, however, came up with her own solution. She bought a Sleep Sheep, a stuffed animal that plays four different sounds of nature and is designed to help soothe children at bedtime. The Sleep Sheep was an immediate hit with the class, and one of the biggest rewards Doris can give a child now is to let him or her choose the sound to signal a transition. Note that if you are hesitant about using an object to signify transitions, other techniques such as singing or clapping a pattern work well and do not involve reliance on an object.

Doris also made a point of keeping her classroom schedule very predictable. This helped the children to anticipate typical transitions throughout the day. As the children were able to anticipate a change, they were able to begin to up- or down-regulate based on the coming activity. This is an important point. While the goal of this resource is to help identify strategies and opportunities to help regulate children, our ultimate goal is to have them be able to *self*-regulate with little or no external input—from their parents or from their teachers.

Working with Parents

For parents inquiring about ways to help their child better manage transitions at home, you might suggest that

Helping Children to Manage Transitions

- if there is going to be a major transition, the parents talk about why it is happening and encourage the child to share his or her feelings about it.

- the parents give as much notice as possible when there will be a change in routine, such as visitors arriving or when an anticipated activity has to be cancelled.

- the parents provide an age-appropriate "countdown" to let the child know how much time he or she has remaining to enjoy an activity; this should lessen the upset experienced when it is time to stop and switch to another activity (e.g., when it is time to stop playing and get ready for bed).

Once Doris began to view her practice through the lens of self-regulation, she became very creative. Surveying her classroom, she recognized that all surfaces, including the floor, had been chosen with an eye to what was easiest to clean. The hardest surfaces, however, also make the most noise, and the sound of a chair or desk scraping across the floor was upsetting to some of the children.

After some creative thinking and a bit of research, Doris came up with several simple solutions to the noise issue. First, she attached tennis balls to the bottom of all classroom desk and chair legs. This helped to soften the noise generated from the class. Taking a cue from her home, Doris installed weather stripping around the classroom door—less to keep out weather in this instance but to help muffle sounds from the hallway.

Doris's next solution involved redefining her classroom's geography. She did an assessment of her centres and placed noise-generating centres—blocks, dramatic play, and sand—in one area of the room. In the other area of the classroom, she placed quiet centres—the library, the writing centre, and the art centre. In this part of the room, she also created a quiet space that was away from direct light where children could simply sit and regroup. Doris helped to define each area by draping white cotton fabric as curtains from wooden dowels—another transition tip for the children.

This left the greatest source of distracting noise—the children! The point of working on the visual and auditory environment was to reduce the sensory overload that certain children found overstimulating. But what other things could be done in the classroom makeover to help those children stay calmly focused and alert?

Classroom Seating

Doris had always set up her classroom with individual desks and chairs organized in groups of six, spaced around the room, all in her sightline. Each year, she gave a great deal of thought to seating arrangements, and had always managed to find the right combination by Thanksgiving. Now, with so many children prone to being hypo- or hyperactive, it was becoming increasingly difficult to find the perfect set-up. Doris decided to tackle the issue on several fronts.

First, her principal, intrigued by the way the classroom was shaping up, gave Doris the green light to follow the occupational therapists' recommendation to buy five disc cushions—inexpensive, air-filled cushions with soft spikes on the bottom and a pebbled pattern on the top. These cushions have proven to be particularly effective with children who have attention or sensory-integration issues (Pfeiffer, Henry, Miller, & Witherell, 2008). Doris was able to use the cushions throughout the day as they were needed; that is, she gave them to children who were having difficulty focusing on learning or who were fidgeting in their seat because they were not comfortable.

Figure 1.3

Disc cushions can be very calming for restless children.

For some time, occupational therapists have told of the benefits of fidget toys, exercise bands, playdough, and worry beads to help children stay calmly focused and alert. Doris decided to have children create their own personal set of worry beads.

She purchased wooden beads (13 to 17 beads per child), shield beads (1 per child), and cord. Children made their own set of worry beads and then personalized them using permanent markers. They now had their own personal set of worry beads that they could use at their desk.

Finally, Doris began to monitor her class, noting points of the day that proved problematic for children when they were hypo- or hyper-aroused. She needed to plan for activities and transitions that would help them to self-regulate. At this point, Doris entered the final phase of her classroom makeover.

Daily Planning Makeover

The self-regulation lens helps us to make sense of what teachers have always been aware of: there is a flux and flow to the day, and there are times despite your best planning when you know that your class is going to be restless and have low energy levels. As some occupational therapists point out, there should be opportunities for exercise in the classroom, especially for students who need more physical activity to restore their energy balance. For some students, lifting a heavy weight or doing some form of heavy exercise has this effect. For others, having them slither about on the floor like a snake, or being as quiet as a mouse, can have a very calming effect.

At times in her classroom day when children were having difficulty with regulation, Doris began instituting some simple exercises (such as doing star jumps) to up-regulate them. Similarly, when the children needed down-regulating, she would use games such as Simon Says to help them to focus.

The techniques discussed so far are designed to regulate a child from the outside, but our ultimate goal is optimal *self*-regulation. The first step in this process is for the *child* to become aware of when he or she is calm, and when he or she is hypo- or hyperaroused. We need to encourage this awareness at the start of the school day.

One of the most important teaching rituals to ease the transition from home to school is to greet each student warmly at the start of the day. This ritual also affords you a wonderful opportunity to assess a child's arousal state. For students, it provides them with a sense of belonging and reinforces the notion that they, as individuals, are recognized and valued by their teacher.

The Alert Program®, designed by occupational therapists Mary Sue Williams and Sherry Shellenberger (1996, 2001, 2006, 2008), is based on the fundamental principles of sensory integration—how the brain helps us to control our body by integrating different kinds of sensations coming from our eyes, ears, mouth, nose, and touch, as well as from our joints, deep muscles, and the position of our limbs. The program's purpose is to teach children, parents, and teachers about self-regulation—what it is, how to identify it, how to articulate one's arousal state, and what sorts of practices help one to become better regulated. The Alert Program® uses an engine analogy and teaches that there are five ways to change arousal states: Mouth, Move, Touch,

The Importance of Physical Activity in Biological Self-Regulation

The first step in optimal self-regulation takes place when the child becomes aware of when he or she is hypo- or hyperaroused.

Alert Program®

Look, and Listen. In the classroom and daily planning makeover, Doris incorporated all of these strategies: Mouth (using deep breaths while singing songs), Move (doing star jumps, moving pile of books, and sitting on disc cushions), Touch (worry beads and playdough), Look (removing visual clutter, dimming or brightening lights), and Listen (using Sleep Sheep, chime in place of the school buzzer, tennis ball on bottom of desk/chair legs, and calming music).

Williams and Shellenberger designed their program to teach children how to learn to regulate themselves and teach teachers how to easily guide the process. In this application, the program uses a simple chart with pictures of three cars on it and is suitable for primary-aged children. One car has an engine that is running "too slow," one has an engine that is running "too fast," and one has an engine that is running "just right."

Figure 1.4

This sample chart was adapted from materials in the book, *"How Does Your Engine Run?"*® *A Leader's Guide to the Alert Program*® *for Self-Regulation* (Williams & Shellenberger, 1996).

Doris created and posted an Alert Program® engine chart in her classroom. She now points to it as each child arrives and asks him or her how his or her engine is running that day. Not surprisingly, all, or almost all, of the children initially answer that their engine is running "just right," even though it might be running too slow or too fast.

Doris helps guide the labelling of their engine speeds and uses a few simple techniques, such as the one listed below, to quickly get them calmly focused and alert.

1. Before class, Doris makes a small pile of books on the floor.

Proprioceptor—a sensory receptor found in muscles, tendons, joints, and the inner ear, which responds to position and movement

2. She asks a child whose engine is running too slowly or too quickly to move the pile of books to the other side of the room (and perhaps "pretend to be an animal"), because she knows that heavy lifting has a calming effect on a child's nervous system. Then the child hops like a bunny or slithers like a snake to move the pile of books. The Alert Program® emphasizes heavy work activities since the **proprioceptors** in joints and muscles help engines to up- or down-regulate (Williams & Shellenberger, 2001).

3. She then asks the child how his engine is running after performing this task. Most children will respond by pointing appropriately to the engine that corresponds to their level of alertness. If he responds, "Now it's just right," when Doris feels the child is still in a hyperaroused state, she helps guide the labelling of his engine speeds. Then throughout the day, Doris brings attention to her own adult "engine" level, by labelling when she herself is in high, low, or just right. She also makes comments in a neutral tone of voice when she sees the child's engine in high, low, or just right: "Looks like your engine is running in low, right now, while you are trying to read your book. Let's do a few star jumps, so your engine will be running just right for reading and concentrating." The next time the child comes in to class, he is likely to be more aware of his own state and what he can do to achieve optimal self-regulation—and to feel better.

Every child is different, of course, and what helps one child to up- or down-regulate might not work for another. So we, as teachers, need to experiment with different techniques to discover what works best for a particular student. The Alert Program® makes this experimentation easy for teachers and supports children to learn the many ways to help their "engines run just right." For example, while some students require physical exercise to help them up-regulate, cognitive stimulation such as reading or watching something humorous may help others to do the same.

©P

The truth is, it feels much better to be calmly focused and alert than to be sluggish or hyper, and it is this feeling that makes the learning involved in *self*-regulation possible. Many children simply do not know what it feels like to be calm, and mastering this initial reflective step is absolutely critical.

Enhancing and Managing Childrens' Self-Regulation During the Rest of the Day

As a teacher, sometimes the most difficult part of getting the children to self-regulate is to recognize how your behaviour can have a regulating effect on them. This might involve lowering your voice and slowing your speech when a student gets agitated, and it certainly would involve becoming more patient. It may also require you to rethink some of your personal routines. For example, one teacher stopped using her favourite hand cream after she discovered that its scent had a dysregulating effect on some students.

Using self-regulation ideas to manage the day is more than a case of building in restorative breaks. Learning activities can be delivered in ways that enhance self-regulation—by providing a choice of engaging activities and a degree of student ownership of their learning. The more students are engaged in an activity, and have a sense of control over their learning, the more likely they are to achieve a state of optimal self-regulation. Even something as simple as combining movement with reading (such as having students imitate the movements of an animal whose name they have just read on the interactive board) can dramatically enhance the effectiveness of a learning activity.

As the children were always quiet when they worked with playdough, Doris became convinced that there was something about manipulating the material that had this calming effect. The science of self-regulation confirms her intuition: highly tactile activities can have a wonderful regulating effect on a child. Always on the lookout for learning opportunities, Doris realized that she had the ingredients for a wonderful self-directed learning experience. It began with the children reading the recipe for making playdough and choosing the colours they wanted, and ended with the creation of a miniature medieval village that was put on display in the school's front hall beside a picture of her class.

Several Ways to Help Children Regulate

Similarly, Doris noticed that the children were generally quieter after music time, and it goes without saying that calming music had the greatest effect. But once she viewed her practice with a lens of self-regulation, Doris realized that she could also use this time to help children who were noise sensitive get used to the sorts of loud noises that they had to deal with in school. The key was to get a really fun rhythm going and then let her students take turns doing things such as ringing a cow bell when they were singing "Old MacDonald Had a Farm" or using a wood block to simulate the sound of a galloping horse.

STRATEGIES SNAPSHOT

Enhancing the Classroom Environment

- Limit extraneous visual material (e.g., bright commercially made borders and posters, mobiles).

- As much as possible, use basic, natural light colours (e.g., cream, tan, grey) in the classroom to have a calming effect.

- Keep clutter to a minimum (e.g., keep items organized in labelled bins, put items not being used out of sight in cupboards, and discard items that you have not used for a year or two).

- Cover the bottom of desk and chair legs with tennis balls if floors are uncarpeted. Glides with felt on the bottom specifically for this purpose are also available for purchase.

- Arrange your classroom so that noisemaking activities are in one area and quiet activities in another. Separate areas by draping white or cream cotton over dowels to act as curtains.

- If your classroom is in a location where outside noise is a problem, keep windows closed as much as possible.

- Install a rubber strip around your classroom door to help reduce hallway noise.

- Avoid the use of noisy fans, and turn computers off when not in use.

- Use natural light as much as possible.

- Plan seating arrangements that will encourage your students to remain calm and focused.

©P

- Provide quiet, calming areas where children can go when they need to down-regulate so that they can focus and be attentive.

Classroom Management

- To reduce the auditory distraction caused by a buzzer, consult with your principal about instituting a chime or music rather than a buzzer to signify school transitions.

- Use objects such as drums, Tibetan gongs, singing bowls, or music (or techniques such as singing or clapping a pattern) to signify in-class transitions.

- Keep your classroom schedule predictable to help students anticipate typical transitions throughout the day.

- Consider using fidget toys, exercise bands, or worry beads to help students stay calmly focused and alert.

- Observe your class over several days. Note times when a number of students seem to have difficulty transitioning from one learning event to another—and need assistance to down- or up-regulate. Consider small changes (e.g., implementing physical activity sessions and games such as Simon Says) between these events and monitor their effectiveness. Observe student reactions, and continue to monitor and adapt to ease transitions.

- Observe your students and note those who experience hypo- or hyperarousal more often and for longer periods than their peers. Keep track of triggers and consider whether you can make modifications to make it easier for students to self-regulate.

- Provide activities that allow for student choice. When students are highly engaged in a learning event, it is easier for them to maintain their focus.

- Make your self-regulation techniques obvious to your students. Use age-appropriate vocabulary that will help them to understand and internalize the concept of self-regulation.

- Try to establish a connection with your students' parents or caregivers and their community so there is continuity between self-regulation strategies used in and out of the classroom.

Chapter 2

The Emotional Domain

Key Attributes of the Emotional Domain

Children who are optimally self-regulated in the emotional domain will demonstrate these key attributes:

- the ability to modulate strong emotions

- emotional resiliency—the ability to recover from disappointment, challenging situations, embarrassment, and other difficulties, and move forward confidently and positively

- willingness and interest to experiment and to learn, on their own and in collaboration with others

- a desire to create and innovate, and while doing so to use a wide range of strategies and techniques

- a healthy self-esteem that is based on awareness of personal efforts and achievements—as well as those of others

Over the last few years, emotional problems in young children have become a major concern to educators, parents, and others. We are seeing increasing numbers of children who are excessively angry or sad, or—every bit as worrying—who barely seem to experience positive emotions such as curiosity, interest, or even just happiness.

©P

It is hard to say why this is happening, but it may be partly due to the speed of change in our society. One worry is that urbanization brings with it all sorts of physical and psychological pressures that stress children and, for that matter, their families. There are also growing and related concerns about the sheer quantity of visual, auditory, and social stimuli that children experience, particularly in urbanized environments; the lack of nature-based experiences; the decline of exercise and organized *and impromptu* sports; changing family patterns and leisure pursuits; and exposure to troubling emotional themes in the news media.

Emotions and Self-Regulation

We could ask why teachers should worry about a child's emotions and how they are regulated. Is that not the responsibility of parents, the extended family, in some cases a spiritual leader, and the larger community? Is it not a teacher's job to develop cognitive skills and teach content, processes, and skills?

The problem with taking that position, as the self-regulation framework that we considered in the last chapter tells us, is that there is a very close connection between children's state of arousal and their ability to learn. As the physiological connections we looked at showed us, the more energy that is needed to up-regulate from a hypoaroused state, or to down-regulate from a hyperaroused state, the fewer resources are available for a child to think clearly and stay focused. The same holds true for the emotional domain. In simple terms, if a child is depressed, frightened, anxious, angry, frustrated, or ashamed, that child will find it very difficult, if not impossible, to concentrate. Conversely, the calmer, happier, safer, and more curious, confident, and interested the child, the better that child will learn.

As an educator, you work hard every day to regulate your students' emotions. It takes a lot of effort to get and keep the students in your classes interested, often by attending to those who need to be calmed. It is not just a case of dealing with students who have a great

Working with Parents

Recent research has shown a correlation between early motor behaviour and social, emotional, and academic-related activity. Of particular interest is "interlimb coordination," the sequential and simultaneous use of both sides of the body with a degree of rhythmicity (Bobbio, Gabbard, & Caçola, 2012). For parents inquiring about ways to help improve their child's motor skills, you might suggest they try to involve the child in some of the following activities:

- clapping, tapping, jumping, or skipping along with music

- playing a keyboard or percussion instrument with both hands

- performing finger plays

- doing jumping jacks

- imitating animals that walk sideways or, for older children, throwing and catching balls while sliding sideways

- playing games involving interlimb coordination, such as hopscotch or Sharks and Minnows

deal of trouble regulating their emotions or, even more challenging, of dealing with a "classroom contagion" effect (the sort of charged emotional current that swiftly spreads through a group of students). The fact is, in a class of 25, for example, a teacher has to deal every day with 25 *different* emotional profiles, 25 students who—on top of all the academic material they are learning—are dealing with a range of emotions that can leave some of them feeling overwhelmed.

Watching the most effective educators in action brings home an important lesson about emotion regulation. These educators seem to have a special gift for understanding their students' and, just as important, their *own* emotional needs. They have a knack for helping students deal with their emotions, and for staying calm themselves in the middle of a maelstrom. Fortunately, *all* educators can learn these skills. And, once learned, such skills will help make teaching the fulfilling profession it should be.

Skeptics may wonder, "What exactly, then, am I supposed to do? Do I become a psychotherapist? Do I go *into* psychotherapy?"

©P

No—our goal here is more modest and practical. It involves a straightforward understanding of the importance of children's emotions in their ability to learn, and emphasizes what educators can *realistically* do to help students optimally regulate those emotions. We will look more closely at such practicalities in some detail later in the chapter. First, though, we need to consider the origins of the long-standing, still dominant, view of how emotions should be regulated.

The Persistence of Long-Established Attitudes

Malcolm Gladwell

In his book *Outliers: The Story of Success*, Malcolm Gladwell (2008) takes the reader on a fascinating journey that shows how cultural attitudes can dominate the behaviour of individuals years after those attitudes were forged. For example, Gladwell points out that researchers were able to show how current male undergraduates at the University of Michigan continued to respond to insults as their feuding ancestors from Harlan, Kentucky (the Howards and the Turners), had done in the 18th century. This behaviour was in contrast to that of their student counterparts with roots in other areas who tended to make light of insults (p. 162).

The same point can be made about still-common views concerning how emotions should be regulated. In this case, however, the sources of these views do not go back just a few generations. They go back more than 2000 years—to Plato!

Plato argued that a teacher's main job with any child was to foster reason-controlled emotional strength, an idea that has been remarkably resilient in one form or another in Western thinking. The ancient Romans, for example, believed that a child could only acquire such strength and mental discipline by being drilled in the rules of grammar and subjected to corporal punishment for any misbehaviour. This belief became the basis of the medieval view of how children should be educated, captured in Figure 2.1, which shows a carving from Chartres Cathedral in France.

©P

Figure 2.1

A stern woman representing Grammar keeps a watchful eye on two young pupils. In her left hand, she holds an open book. In her right hand, she holds a flagellum, or whip.

It is helpful to consider how our attitudes toward a student's emotion regulation and its role in learning are still influenced by these long-established attitudes. Questions worth asking ourselves in this regard include the following:

Dealing with Our Own Emotions (Parenting When We Are Upset)

- How irritated, even angry, do I become with a child who cannot control his emotions, and especially, his anger?

- Do I feel that a child who cannot control her emotions needs to learn that she will suffer serious consequences if she chooses to give in to her emotions?

- Do I feel that giving in to this child's outbursts is a sign of weakness on my part?

- Can I actually help this child to keep her emotions in check? Do I think that I can't do so or that this child is simply beyond help?

Note how questions such as the above reflect a generally negative view of emotions (the very word *emotional* often has negative connotations). They leave out any consideration that emotions might, in fact, play an important and useful self-regulating function in human behaviour.

©P

The Regulating Role of Emotions

Let us begin by emphasizing a very critical point:

> *Emotion regulation is as much about up-regulating positive emotions as it is about down-regulating negative ones.*

Not surprisingly, and as research has confirmed (Lawson, 2002), excessive negative emotions can be highly damaging to a child's mental health. This should not, however, colour our view of *all* emotions. Positive emotions are essential, not only for activating and energizing actions, but also for sparking and sustaining the attention necessary for learning to occur.

Furthermore, there is often a dynamic interplay between regulating positive and negative emotions. For instance, a child can be both enthusiastic and a bit anxious or fearful about learning to skate. What she needs to do is learn how to harness her positive feeling of enthusiasm to deal with her negative feeling of anxiety (for example, by thinking, "It will be fun, so I shouldn't worry"). If she gives in to her fear, she will probably come up with an excuse to avoid trying to skate, even though she would very much like to.

The truth is, as an educator, you cannot ignore a student's emotions and how they are regulated. If a student has to make a great effort to try to remain calm, she might have little remaining energy to attend to what you are saying. If another student deals with his feelings of distress or anxiety by withdrawal, he is probably cutting himself off from learning opportunities. Very simply, the *development of children's cognitive abilities is fundamentally dependent on how well children function emotionally*. The developmental origins of this intimate connection of the emotional and the cognitive is the focus of the groundbreaking research done by Stanley Greenspan.

Emotions and Learning

"Positive emotions such as joy, contentment, acceptance, trust and satisfaction can enhance learning. Conversely, prolonged emotional distress can cripple our ability to learn. We all know how hard it is to learn or remember something when we are anxious, angry or depressed."

— Lawson, 2002, para. 4

The Greenspan Floortime Approach

The Link Between Emotions, Behaviour, and Learning

Greenspan's Theory of Emotional Development

In his extensive research on very young children over the years, Greenspan (1979, 1981, 1989, 1993) came to recognize that emotion regulation begins very early with the differentiation between, and the communication of, emotions. Subsequently, Greenspan saw that

Affect Signals—non-verbal means we use to indicate our emotions or mood, including tone of voice, gestures, and facial expressions (such as a smile or annoyed look)

Responding to Negative Emotions

"Our higher-level language and thinking, including theory of mind, are founded upon our basic abilities for attention and sequencing. Early emotional interactions help a child learn to pay attention and plan and sequence action."

— **Greenspan & Shanker, 2004, pp. 260–261**

emotion regulation hinges on the development of emotional awareness and self-reflection. On the basis of his clinical observations, Greenspan concluded that between 18 and 24 months of age, children develop two critical abilities:

- the ability to *communicate* their negative emotions through purposeful **affect signals** rather than through visceral, unfocused, hyperaroused behaviour, such as tantrums

- the ability to *modulate* their emotions (that is, to down- or up-regulate them) as a result of caregivers' responses to their behaviour (that is, as a result of caregivers regulating their behaviour)

In Greenspan's view—further developed in later work (Greenspan & Shanker, 2004)—the development of purposeful communication skills changes the very way in which a child views his or her ability to tackle situations that he or she has to this point found overwhelming. In other words, a child's knowledge that she has a tool that can help her stay calm instills in her the confidence that can help her deal with potentially disruptive emotions, ones that could drain her energy and make her less able to cope with difficult situations.

Implications of Greenspan's Research for the Classroom

Greenspan's theory has very important implications, highlighted below, for how you might approach emotion regulation in the classroom.

We cannot ignore the emotional dimension of students' behaviour if we want to maximize their potential for learning.
This point cannot be emphasized enough, and is as true for the student who is having trouble experiencing positive emotions as for the student who has trouble regulating his or her anger or frustration. As noted at the beginning of this chapter, this does not mean that a teacher needs to serve as a therapist for a student. Rather, teachers need to ask themselves why they are seeing these problems. What, in other words, might be triggering them?

Working with Parents

For parents inquiring about ways to help their child better self-regulate at home, you might suggest that they

- provide as predictable a routine as possible

- let their child take responsibility for tasks, and for monitoring their own success at completing each task

- help relieve the child's stress by making them aware of upcoming transitions

- model self-regulation in their own behaviour

Emotion regulation is intimately connected with the other four domains. Obviously, the more hyper- or hypoaroused a student is, the more vulnerable he or she will be to problems in emotion regulation. Less obvious are the ways in which the cognitive, social, and prosocial realms are connected with such regulation. As we will see in later chapters, the more difficulty a student has in a realm (for example, in the cognitive realm, finding a particular sort of problem challenging; in the social domain, having difficulty interacting appropriately with others in the playground; or in the prosocial realm, having difficulty acquiring a sense of right and wrong), the more prone he or she will be to frustration and anxiety, or to sadness and low self-esteem.

Discipline involving fear of reprisal does not enhance emotional self-regulation.
As noted on page 25, long-standing views about regulating children "from the outside" commonly involve fear of reprisal. Such an approach does not encourage sustained self-regulation because it is largely dependent on the presence of an authority figure such as a teacher or parent. In addition, fear (or other negative emotions such as anxiety or anger) can push certain children into a hyper- or hypoaroused state from which they may find it difficult to recover.

Harsh Discipline Does Not Enhance Emotional Self-Regulation

We need to always think about how we can enhance students' emotional self-regulation.

It is tempting to restrict our thinking to what *we* can do to regulate a student's emotions. While "external" regulation is often a starting point, it should be no more than a means to encouraging students to regulate their own emotions.

We need to incorporate a range of learning activities in the classroom that allow all students to showcase their strengths.

Not all students are adept at traditional, language-based activities and assessments. This is particularly true when working with students who have language-based learning disabilities or who are English Language Learners. Providing opportunities for students to develop and showcase their knowledge through other means—art, music, and technology as examples—bolsters their self-worth and offers us an opportunity to reinforce their confidence.

We need to vary our groupings so that students work with a range of classmates and in a range of working styles.

While some classroom work necessarily involves ability groupings, we can look for ways to mix groups of students so that they have an opportunity to work with others of varying abilities. While care needs to be taken when mixing groups (for example, avoiding placing lower-achieving students in an environment in which they are expected to work on level with higher-achieving peers), activities in all subject areas can be designed to include mixed-ability groupings. In addition, we can allow students the chance to work in a range of situations—individually, with a partner, and as part of a group. Some students are hesitant in group settings and will get more positive reinforcement when working on their own or with a trusted partner.

We need to shift our focus from an emphasis on product to the learning process.

A child who is optimally regulated in the emotional domain has confidence in his or her ability as a learner. We need to ensure that we help students to broaden their scope—and our scope—of what constitutes effective learning and learning strengths. Too often in our classrooms, we place emphasis on a student's completed piece of work, whether it be a history project, a quiz, or a standardized test. When we step back and consider our students' learning on an

©P

ongoing basis, we can identify strengths in areas beyond the traditional scope, for example, identifying a student's creative use of a learning strategy, or his or her ability to motivate group members as they work through a difficult assignment. Such strengths—being a creative problem solver or being skilled at motivating others, for example—are increasingly valued in the workplace.

We need to become very reflective about our own emotion regulation. This means becoming more aware of our own emotions and how we regulate them, even as we try to up- or down-regulate the various emotions of the students in our classes.

Applications in the Classroom

Scenario

Kyle was in his first job and he had been thrown in at the deep end: he had been hired to teach a Grade 6 class in which many of the students were having problems regulating their emotions. Some students would get frightened, anxious, or angry at the slightest provocation and find it difficult to calm down. Others were so totally tuned out that Kyle could not reach them at all. What disturbed him most was how detached so many seemed to be from their emotional lives. He wondered whether watching too much television or playing too many violent video games was numbing them to the subtleties and complexities of their emotional lives—a question many of us ask today.

Kyle came to speak to me after a workshop in which I had talked about the five-domain model of self-regulation, which we looked at in the Introduction. He wanted to learn more about the emotional domain because he was worried about what he called the "emotional illiteracy" of his students.

I suggested to Kyle that he check the websites of Daniel Goleman and the Collaborative for Academic, Social, and Emotional Learning (CASEL).

Daniel Goleman

Collaborative for Academic, Social, and Emotional Learning (CASEL)

Emotional Intelligence and Social Emotional Learning: Their Roots and Effects

While it may seem that Daniel Goleman originated the theory of emotional intelligence, it was, in fact, the work of two psychologists, Peter Salovey and John Mayer, whose early work Goleman spotted as a science reporter for the *New York Times*. Fascinated with the notion that emotional intelligence—a person's ability to identify and analyze personal emotions and then respond in a way that exerts control—could rival IQ as an indicator of success, Goleman made the exploration and writing of this intriguing field his focus.

Goleman's work on emotional intelligence has had a powerful effect on the field. His model identifies four main elements of emotional intelligence:

- Self-awareness—the ability to identify one's own emotions
- Self-management—the ability to modulate one's emotions
- Social awareness—the ability to understand others' emotions
- Relationship management—the ability to co-regulate and manage interpersonal conflicts

Interpersonal Relationships

Thanks in large part to Goleman's work, emotional intelligence now forms the cornerstone of social and emotional learning (SEL) initiatives at the school level. These programs aim to help children and youth develop enduring traits that will benefit their social, emotional, and intellectual well-being.

The Collaborative for Academic, Social, and Emotional Learning (CASEL) is a U.S.-based organization that promotes the teaching of SEL in schools around the world. Recently, CASEL took part in a meta-analysis of more than 200 studies of programs focused on youth development, character education, SEL, and prevention intervention—involving some 270 000 students from Kindergarten through Grade 12.

Among CASEL's findings, these programs were shown to

- be effective in both school and after-school settings and for students with and without behavioural and emotional problems
- be effective for racially and ethnically diverse students from urban, rural, and suburban settings across the K–12 grade range

- improve students' social-emotional skills, attitudes about self and others, connection to school, and positive social behaviour; and to reduce conduct problems and emotional distress
- improve students' achievement test scores by 11 percentile points (Durlak, Weissberg, Dymnicki, Taylor, & Schellinger, 2011, p. 405)

The Impact of Students' Social and Emotional Learning

I heard from Kyle again after he had carefully reviewed the different materials on the CASEL website. While he had found some good program ideas, he was unsure of how to introduce the topic to the 12-year-olds in his class, many of whom were new to Canada and came from a wide variety of cultural and linguistic backgrounds. Together we decided to work out a personalized "Course in Emotion Regulation" that would make the students eager to learn about their emotions and how best to regulate them to maximize their learning.

Developing an Emotional Language

Teaching Emotion Regulation

Kyle started by asking his students what an emotion is. He was surprised by the superficiality and consistency of their responses. They answered his question by giving him an example of an emotion. When pressed to dig deeper (for example, to tell him what "happiness" is), they responded, "It's when you feel good." When asked how they could tell if someone else is happy, they would typically answer that you really could not tell unless it was a close friend.

This led Kyle and me to think about whether this "course" should only be about helping students to monitor and modulate their emotions. Why not turn it into a unique learning opportunity? This is an important point that needs to be highlighted: *working on self-regulation in this and other domains should not be seen as a separate item in the curriculum.* Everything you do, every class activity, offers an opportunity to enhance self-regulation; and the more self-regulation is enhanced, the more successful that learning is going to be.

Moreover, research has shown that, just as the parts of the brain that govern self-regulation keep maturing right up until the early 20s, so too do the emotional skills needed to cope with increasingly complex emotional challenges (ACT for Youth, 2002). Therefore, constantly helping students to develop emotion-regulating skills should be a core element in our teaching mindset and toolkit.

"Until recently most scientists believed that the major 'wiring' of the brain was completed by as early as three years of age…. New findings show that the greatest changes to the parts of the brain that are responsible for functions such as self-control, judgment, emotions, and organization occur between puberty and adulthood."

— **ACT for Youth, 2002, para. 1**

Adolescent Brain Development

Emotions in Animals

A scientist at heart, Kyle was familiar with Darwin's theory of emotions. He began his course with this simple question: "Do animals have emotions?" The question immediately engaged his students.

Drawing on Darwin's argument that animals have their own versions of the emotions we experience, Kyle created his first assignment. Students were asked to find examples of animal emotions on the internet.

Animal Planet

Kyle had expected his students to cite clips from the media showing animals that were happy or frightened or angry. But it was not just movies on YouTube that had caught their attention; they were also scouring the blogs, including those on the Animal Planet website.

Kyle remained intent on focusing his students' attention on the scientific questions that Darwin raised, framed in a way that his students would understand:

- Why might we see emotions in animals similar to those we see in humans?

- Where do these emotions come from?

- What role do "animal-like" emotions play in the lives of humans?

- Do all humans have the same emotions?

This last question turned out to be particularly provocative for Kyle's culturally diverse class. The students were given the opportunity to talk about what their family regarded as the most important emotions. Soon all of the students were engaged in a homework assignment in which they had to describe what their family or community regarded as the most important emotions.

Basic Human Emotions

Following the homework assignment on the most important emotions, Kyle returned to the big question: Are there certain *basic* emotions that all humans have, and if so, what are they? This gave the class the opportunity to study what they look like when they are happy, sad, or angry. In one particularly productive classroom discussion, students quickly came up with individual lists of what they thought were the eight basic emotions, and then compared their lists for similarities and differences. All students had *anger, fear, happiness, love,* and *sadness* on

 ©P

their list. Many listed *surprise*, and quite a few had *embarrassment* (or *shame*). After that, however, there was a great deal of variation.

The most common of the miscellaneous emotions identified by the students were *boredom*, *contempt*, *disappointment*, *guilt*, *hurt*, *helplessness*, *humiliation*, *intimidation*, *jealousy*, *loneliness*, *pride*, and *resentment*. What really struck Kyle, and you have perhaps noticed it also, is that this list of emotions is almost entirely negative. Only one student in the entire class had listed *hopefulness*.

In the following class, Kyle talked about Paul Ekman and Wallace Friesen's idea (2003) that all people start off with the same "hard-wired" facial expressions for seven basic emotions (happiness, sadness, anger, fear, surprise, disgust, and contempt). This led to a discussion of why some students in the class were taught from a very young age not to show such emotions. Further discussion covered other issues involved in emotions, such as how each basic emotion consists of a distinctive feeling, a particular facial expression and posture, and special kinds of movements and posture. For example, happiness is characterized by a feeling of contentment, a wide smile, a raising of the corners of the lips, a bulging of the cheeks, and a crinkling of the corners of the eyes.

What Kyle really wanted his students to start thinking about was how basic, or "programmed," emotional responses were (a) triggered in much the same way as the pupils of eyes suddenly dilating in a dark room, and (b) passed on from one generation to the next because of the functions they served.

When Kyle asked his students what functions they thought basic emotional responses served, answers included the following:

- "Fear is an automatic response I have to danger."

- "Disgust protects me from eating something that might make me sick."

- "Anger gives me the physical energy I need to win a game."

- "Curiosity makes me want to explore things around me, like nature or a new app on my phone."

Dr. Paul Ekman

"Research has shown that accurate judgments of emotion can be made from the rapid facial signals, and has recently uncovered the particular facial signals—the blueprints—which distinguish each of the primary emotions."

— Ekman & Friesen, 2003, p. 11

Emotion Regulation

Kyle was now ready to start talking about emotion regulation and why it is so important. He first had to explain to the class how these programmed emotional responses are like reflexes that kick in when particular situations arise.

Kyle then asked:

- Have you ever had an emotional response that wasn't appropriate to a situation? For example, have you ever laughed when someone told you a sad story?

- Have you ever felt that your emotional response was out of proportion to what prompted it? For example, have you ever become really angry over something small?

- Have you ever found it very hard to calm down after you have been really upset?

- Do you sometimes think that you don't feel the same emotions as your classmates? For example, have you ever seen everyone else really excited about something, such as a field trip, but did not feel that way yourself?

- Do you sometimes feel that your emotions are all over the place? For example, have you ever felt really happy one moment, and very angry a minute later?

After discussing these questions, it was time for the next phase: personalizing the "science" of emotion regulation.

The Power of the Arts in Personalizing Emotion Regulation

Reading About Emotions

Kyle had always loved reading to his class, putting on different voices and asking his students probing questions about the story they had just read. To enhance their exploration of emotion regulation, Kyle decided to select, display, and read books and stories specifically for the discussion about emotions that they encouraged. Soon students were freely responding to the emotions of the characters in the stories that Kyle read to them and that they read on their own.

Developing Self-Awareness of Emotion Regulation

Step 1: Snapshots of Emotions
In order to develop student self-awareness of emotion regulation, Kyle began with a homework assignment. Arrangements were made for the students to borrow inexpensive digital cameras to take home and use to photograph their parents pretending to be happy, sad, angry, afraid, interested, surprised, and disgusted. When the images had been printed out, Kyle asked his students to identify which emotions their parents were feeling, and then to look at photographs of their classmates' parents and try to identify *their* emotions. It was fascinating for the students to see how much more difficult it was to identify other parents' emotions than those of their own parents. For example, a couple of the fathers scowled very convincingly when pretending to be angry, while other dads only compressed their lips slightly and narrowed their eyes.

Reading Faces

Afterwards, Kyle had his students talk among themselves to find out how they guessed which emotions other parents were feeling. What made them think that someone else's father was showing anger when it looked like he was showing no emotion at all? They were quickly learning a lesson in how hard it can be to know what someone else is feeling when you do not know that person well.

Step 2: Drawing a "Wheel of Basic Emotions"
Next, Kyle had his students draw a "Wheel of Basic Emotions," an idea borrowed from reading Robert Plutchik (1980). The wheel would be in the form of an eight-slice pie chart to accommodate the following basic emotions: joy, trust, fear, surprise, sadness, disgust, anger, and anticipation. Students were then asked to decide which of these emotions they thought were most closely connected to each other, and to place them accordingly in the pie chart (for example, should fear go next to anger, or surprise next to anticipation). They were then to compare their wheels.

Step 3: Identifying Gradations in the Emotions
Kyle asked his students to think of as many stages (or gradations) as they could for each of the eight emotions, from mild to very intense states, and to record them in a chart similar to Figure 2.2.

Figure 2.2: Gradations of Emotions Chart

Emotion	Mild	Gradations	Very Intense
Joy	delight		ecstasy
Trust	comfort		dependence
Fear	apprehension		terror
Surprise	distraction		astonishment
Sadness	gloominess		grief
Disgust	dislike		repulsion
Anger	annoyance		fury
Anticipation	attentiveness		enthrallment

Next, Kyle had his students look closely at Plutchik's gradations (Figure 2.3) and consider the following questions:

- How do your gradations of emotions compare with these?

- Based on your own emotional experiences, are there any revisions that you would like to make to your wheel after looking at the gradations here?

- Are there any emotions on the wheel that you have never experienced?

- Have you ever experienced two or more gradations of emotions at the same time (for example, feeling dejected and frightened when you were irritated)?

- Have you ever skipped over any of the gradations of an emotion when experiencing that emotion (for example, going from annoyance to fury in a flash)?

 ©P

Figure 2.3: Plutchik's Gradations

The point of the three steps that Kyle used to develop self-awareness of emotion regulation was to help his students develop the communicative tools needed to express the degrees of an emotion. This is critical because clear and purposeful communication of emotions being experienced is essential if a child is to avoid instinctive, unfocused behaviour. Furthermore, for such communication to be fully effective, it must be informed by a child's *awareness of changes* in his or her emotions (for example, a child being conscious of how quickly she is becoming annoyed, or how her anger is starting to turn into rage). To help develop such awareness, Kyle thought of three things: yoga, SNAP, and journal writing.

Step 4: Ways to Heighten Emotional Awareness
Yoga: A dedicated yoga practitioner himself, Kyle read the research showing how beneficial yoga is for children (Wenig, 1999), so he decided to introduce a 20-minute yoga break a few times a week. He immediately noticed that the physicality of the poses had a

"When children learn techniques for self-health, relaxation, and inner fulfillment, they can navigate life's challenges with a little more ease. Yoga at an early age encourages self-esteem and body awareness with a physical activity that's noncompetitive."
— **Wenig, 1999, para. 2**

Yoga for Kids

SNAP (Stop Now and Plan)

wonderfully calming effect on his students. What he had not expected, however, was how enthusiastic his students would become about the meditation part, during which they became especially conscious of their actions and feelings. For example, many commented on how surprised they were to discover that they had been feeling a little afraid or angry. It soon became a bit of a school joke about how everyone could always tell when the Grade 6 students were in their meditating lotus position because of the loud "Ommmmm" echoing down the school halls!

SNAP: Now was also the perfect time for Kyle to introduce his students to SNAP (Stop Now and Plan), the cognitive behavioural strategy developed at the Child Development Institute in Toronto. SNAP coaches children to insert a pause in their automatic, or "programmed," stimulus-response reactions so that they can think of an alternative action before lashing out verbally or physically.

SNAP Steps

STOP—"Things I can do to STOP myself (calm my body) from making problems bigger."

- Snap my fingers (helps to cue me to use stop/calming strategies)
- Take deep breaths
- Put my hands in my pockets
- Take a step back
- Count to 10

NOW, AND—"Things I can say to myself to keep calm and help me to make the right choice."

- Calming thoughts/coping statements
- "This is hard but I can do it."
- "I can stay in control."

PLAN—"Once I have stopped and calmed down, what can I do?"

Pick a plan that will work for me, one that will

- make me feel like a winner
- make the problem smaller not bigger
- not hurt anyone, myself, or anything

Source: The Canadian Safe School Network, n.d.; Child Development Institute

©P

Keeping a Journal: Heightening emotional awareness also involved each student keeping an "Emotion Regulation Journal." In these, the students wrote about their day and about the emotions—positive and negative, intense and otherwise—that they experienced in different situations. To make this exercise both appealing and effective, Kyle explained to his students the kinds of questions about events and related emotions they could mention in their journals. For example:

On first waking up: Was I feeling exhausted? Was I excited or unenthusiastic about going to school?

Breakfast: Did I enjoy it or not? Was I happy to talk to my family?

Before heading to school: Did I feel organized or overwhelmed when getting my stuff together?

At start of school: Did I feel happy about seeing my friends? A bit frustrated about an assignment to be handed in?

Classes: Was I excited by or bored with them?

First recess: Did I feel great relief at the break from class work, or was I still worried about something that happened in class or at home? Did I feel afraid when I saw a bully come my way?

Recesses and lunch: Did I enjoy these breaks or not, including the company of friends?

Gym class: Did I feel good or not about how I performed?

On getting back home: Was I happy or not to be back?

Dinner at home: Was I interested in a story a family member told? Did I become angry at something my mom or dad said to me?

After dinner: Did I become relaxed or tense watching TV or playing a video game?

Going to bed: Did I enjoy reading a book or magazine? Did I become anxious about having to play hockey or another team sport the next day? Did I fall asleep easily?

For each negative emotion they recorded, students could explain what, if anything, they did to get over it. Lastly, they could describe the best and worst things that had happened to them that day, explain why, and highlight the emotions involved and how they coped with them.

As an exercise in developing reflective thinking on both emotions and writing skills, the journal worked extremely well. The students were never asked to show what they had written, but they were encouraged to talk about the most important aspects they were learning from keeping their journal. The message that came through loud and clear was that the more stressed they were, the harder their day was for them emotionally, and the harder it was for them to calm down or get to sleep. The more they had exercised during the day, and the fewer television programs they watched or video games they played, the less impulsive they were and the better they were at self-regulating their emotions. Kyle's students were beginning to understand their personal temperaments and the sorts of activities that helped them to calm down, or conversely, to become focused and alert.

Strategies for Helping Children Deal with Negative Emotions

Working with Parents

For parents inquiring about ways to help their child better cope with frustration and other negative emotions at home, you might suggest that they

- encourage the child to talk freely about what he or she is feeling frustrated about

- role-play with the child what happened to cause the frustration and appropriate ways for dealing with it

- help the child to recognize the signs his or her body sends when feelings of frustration or anger first start (for example, gritted teeth, tense body, pounding heart, clenched fists), so feelings can be controlled before they get out of hand

- encourage appropriate physical activity

Supporting Emotional Development with Positive Emotions

Kyle's Lesson
When Kyle was asked at the end of the year what he felt was the most important lesson he had learned from his class focus on emotion regulation, he answered,

I realized how much my own view of emotion regulation needed to change. At the beginning, I assumed that regulating children's emotions was just about controlling their anger. I had never thought about the other emotions, about how it's just as important to up-regulate their positive emotions as to down-regulate the negative ones. Maybe that's because I used to be so uncomfortable around anger. It was easy for me to comfort a child when she was frightened, or to encourage a child when he was frustrated. But whenever a child became angry, a sort of cold feeling seemed to take over me and, before I knew it, I was responding angrily myself. Now I find that I can remain just as calm in the face of their anger as around all their other emotions.

Kyle reports that he now looks at his students' emotional lives with new eyes. He no longer views his students as simply "undisciplined," and is no longer annoyed by their outbursts or stubbornness. Instead, he now constantly asks himself *why* certain children are behaving in emotionally unsettled ways, or what emotional upset might be getting in the way of his connecting with a particular child. What really matters in the end, he concludes, are not so much the answers that a teacher comes up with as the carefully considered questions that he or she asks.

The Optimistic Child by Dr. Martin Seligman details effective strategies for working with children of all ages who are prone to negative thinking (and depression), getting them to "catch" negative thoughts and turn them around.

A new study from Illinois finds teachers need more professional development to deal effectively with their students' emotions (Rebora, 2012).

Dealing Effectively with Student Emotions

STRATEGIES SNAPSHOT

Encouraging Emotion Regulation

- Be conscious of your emotions and attempts to self-regulate throughout the day.

- Acquaint yourself with the many resources on emotional self-regulation (e.g., videos, reports, tips) appropriate for the age of your students that are offered on websites such as CASEL, Edutopia, and the Canadian Safe School Network (SNAP program). These will help your students develop the key attributes of optimal emotional self-regulation that are listed at the beginning of this chapter.

- Look for ways to encourage the development of emotion regulation throughout the day—do not teach it in isolation. For example:

    – encourage cooperation, tolerance, and respect whenever your students are working in pairs or small groups in *any* subject area and when they are playing in the playground

- raise awareness of emotion-related content in any material your students are reading, writing, role-playing, and so on.

- Consider—and be sensitive to—how your students' cultural and/or social backgrounds may affect their awareness of emotions and attempts at emotion regulation.

- If possible, introduce yoga, tai chi, breathing exercises, or meditation to your class as a way to regulate emotions.

- Help your students learn to express how they are feeling verbally so they will be less likely to act out physically.

- Model self-regulation for your students when faced with frustrating situations in the classroom. For example, try to focus on the emotion that may be driving a student to misbehave rather than on the misbehaviour itself. Your students *will* notice such co-regulating practices.

- When possible, involve families in students' attempts at emotion regulation by, for example, discussing the benefits of their child spending more time being physically active and reading and less time watching television and playing video games.

Chapter 3

The Cognitive Domain

Key Attributes of the Cognitive Domain

Among the many key attributes of the cognitive domain are the abilities to

- focus, and switch focus, as required

- consider perspectives other than one's own

- plan and execute several steps in a row, including being able to try different courses of action when an initial plan has failed to work

- understand cause and effect

- think logically

- set learning goals

- monitor and assess performance

- see that failure provides an opportunity to learn

- manage time effectively

- develop self-awareness, especially the recognition of personal learning strengths and weaknesses

- use learning aids, including digital technologies, where appropriate (e.g., making an outline to help order thoughts in writing)

What Is Cognitive Self-Regulation and Why Is It Important?

Cognition can be defined as the process by which knowledge is obtained. Understandably, then, of the five domains, educators are likely most interested in regulation in the cognitive domain, the area of greatest relevance to the classroom.

Historically, educational psychologists working in the area of self-regulation have been primarily interested in those attributes in the above list that relate to a child's **executive functions** and those metacognitive skills that are highly relevant for learning.

Executive functions are a set of cognitive processes that regulate a number of areas, including planning, working memory (the ability to keep information in mind and use it as needed), problem solving, mental flexibility, and multi-tasking. Researchers in the area of self-regulation have identified executive function skills as being critically important for early academic achievement (Molfese et al., 2010).

Metacognition is the awareness and understanding of one's own thinking or cognitive processes—in simple terms, it is "thinking about thinking." Metacognitive knowledge is commonly thought to consist of three components: knowledge of self (for example, knowing that you learn much better in a quiet setting than a noisy one); knowledge of task (for example, knowing that it is easier to prepare for a multiple-choice test than one that involves a lot of writing); and knowledge of learning strategies (for example, knowing what strategies are suitable for a task and how to use them) (Flavell, 1979).

As important as executive functions and metacognition are for self-regulated learning, we will be primarily concerned in this chapter with a more basic cognitive step that enables a student to develop these skills: namely, the student's ability to process the myriad visual, auditory, tactile, kinesthetic, and propioceptive stimuli (to name just the primary ones) bombarding his or her senses. More precisely, our concern is with this very practical question: *Can a better understanding of the nature of these core processes help us to devise classroom activities that will enhance our students' ability to focus attention and become self-regulated learners?*

To answer that question, we have to get beyond thinking that the following behaviours in children merely reflect a lack of self-discipline or mental strength:

- difficulty focusing attention
- giving up at the slightest frustration

Executive Functions—cognitive processes that regulate areas such as planning, working memory, problem solving, mental flexibility, and multi-tasking

Metacognition—the awareness and understanding of one's own thinking or cognitive processes

©P

- fantasizing unduly

- vulnerability to distracting impulsive thoughts

As noted earlier, such thinking has traditionally been coupled with disciplinary measures that usually do not work with students, precisely because they exacerbate problems in other domains of our five-domain model of self-regulation (biological, emotional, social, and prosocial). It is for this reason that punishing children can, in fact, make their difficulties with attention considerably worse.

Understanding Attention and the Ability to Process

Attention Is Not a Static Phenomenon

Consider the following important questions:

- How do we engage a child's attention in the first place?

- How do we enhance a child's capacity for *sustained optimal attention*?

- How do we support children who find it difficult to disengage themselves from a topic or activity?

- Are some children born with biological problems in their nervous system that can constrict their ability to pay attention? If so, is there anything that can be done in the classroom to help these children learn to focus attention?

- Do some children find it particularly difficult to focus attention when surrounded by other children?

- Why does it seem that many more children have attention problems today than just a decade ago? Are some aspects of media or other elements of modern life having a damaging effect on children's ability to focus attention? (See "Video Games and Natural Opiates," next page.)

- Can current early learning initiatives in several Canadian provinces help reverse these trends? See "The Cognitive Value of Play."

SPOTLIGHT

Video Games and Natural Opiates

Biederman and Vessel (2006) have published an important study on the pleasurable "fix" of natural opiates that are released when we solve a problem. Their research raises the possibility that the more time one spends playing certain video games, the more time playing will be required in subsequent sessions to reach the same level of enjoyment. This, in turn, might reduce the pleasure experienced in less stimulus-rich activities such as reading.

Perceptual Pleasure and the Brain

Classroom Management Tools: Attention Getters

To be sure, consistency is very important in helping to answer many of the questions above. This means using teaching and learning techniques consistently so that students know what to expect and can focus accordingly. However, such techniques do not work with all students. For reasons that we looked at in Chapter 1, certain techniques, such as using a loud bell or buzzer to get attention, can actually exacerbate attention problems in some students. Furthermore, as every teacher knows, there is a world of difference between *getting* a student's attention and *keeping* it. The key here is to recognize that attention is not a static phenomenon, like the shutter mechanism on a camera. It cannot be sufficiently emphasized that attention is an active, goal-directed phenomenon in which the student takes in and processes many different kinds of information, and then plans and executes his or her actions accordingly.

The Cognitive Value of Play

A common thread in many early learning initiatives is the promotion of play as an essential element in early learning and development. The need to make a case for play arose when the academic aspect of early learning began to be emphasized. Unfortunately, recognition of the amazing potential for learning in the years from infancy onwards has set up a false dichotomy between learning and play, creating what some have labelled as a crisis in Kindergarten (Miller & Almon, 2009).

This crisis results largely from a misunderstanding about the cognitive value of play in the early years (and beyond) and the strong connection it has to the development of self-regulation in young children. Curiosity, exuberance, and receptivity are critical elements in the connections between play and self-regulation (Ontario Ministry of Children and Youth Services, 2007). When play activities are self-initiated and authentic, children have the motivation to independently generate strategies to sustain the play.

Socio-dramatic play evolves from children's random and self-initiated interactions with materials, toys, and one another on the playground and in various play areas (blocks, sand and water, dramatic play). In this type of scenario, one or two children collaboratively begin to "stage" a drama—their marbles become warriors; they build a castle and a moat to defend their kingdom; they create a family "drama"; they create a racetrack for their individual cars to compete. Typically, the drama evolves with major players who structure the "scenes," like playwrights and stage directors. Children "become" the characters, transforming available materials for their dramatic purposes.

This play is authentic and meaningful to children. In structuring these dramatic play scenarios, they are independently engaged in many of the essential elements of cognitive development. Children have an investment in self-regulating to maintain the play, to keep it moving forward. To do that, they engage in a sophisticated dance, matching their own intrinsic interests/goals in the games while being sensitive to the interests of others so that they, too, will be motivated to continue the play.

The New Brunswick document (2008) identifies "Play and Playfulness" as one of four essential goals for children's early learning and care (along with Well-Being, Communication and Literacies, and Diversity and Social Responsibility).

Early Learning Initiatives

"Play is a vehicle for learning and lies at the core of innovation and creativity. It provides opportunities for learning in a context in which children are at their most receptive."

— **Ontario Ministry of Education, 2010–11, p. 13.**

"Children in play-based kindergartens have a double advantage over those who are denied play: they end up equally good or better at reading and other intellectual skills, and they are more likely to become well-adjusted healthy people."

— **Miller & Almon, 2009, p. 8**

This type of play can become lively (the New Brunswick Framework labels this "dizzy play") and children may become frustrated when left on their own to problem solve difficult "building" challenges, dramatic interruptions, and social conflicts. This is when the role of adults is critical. If adults step in too quickly, however, they can eliminate the essential value the play has for helping children develop strategies for problem solving and logical thinking. Adults need to be sensitive so they do not interfere with children's creativity and problem-solving ability, as well as the sense of self-worth and confidence that comes from this type of independent self-regulation.

What about children who have difficulty with this type of play? These are the children who most need and would most benefit from this type of play experience. The nature of adult intervention is critical. According to Berk, Mann, and Ogan (2006), children benefit most when adults are "available" to engage in and support the children's self-directed play, interrupting the play only when it becomes anti-social. This might be the time when the engine metaphor introduced in Chapter 1 (page 16) could be useful. Adults could stop the play briefly asking, "How are your engines running right now? Too fast? Too slow? What could you do to get your engines running just right so you can continue playing? Who has some ideas?"

The success of all of this rests on the inherent benefits this type of play has for encouraging creativity and imagination, and for the sense of self-worth that emerges when children are free to explore in open and flexible environments. The recognition of the importance of self-regulation in all aspects of learning may help us take a fresh look at children's play, seeing it as the ultimate laboratory for ALL children to practise and perfect their cognitive abilities across all domains.

— **Pat Dickinson**

"An extensive literature review on play training, mostly conducted with low-SES pre-schoolers, reveals that children with weak play skills who receive adult encouragement to engage in make-believe, relative to alternative-activity or no-play controls, show gains in sociodramatic play, imaginativeness of play content, mental test scores, impulse control, coherence of storytelling, and capacity to empathize with others."

— **Berk, Mann, & Ogan, 2006, p. 92**

©P

Why Do Some Children Have Difficulty Focusing Attention?

There are three basic principles of optimal self-regulation as it applies to focusing attention:

- Children need to be supported as they develop their ability to focus attention.

- Focusing attention is taxing, and more so for some children than others.

- Focusing attention requires fine-tuning and harmonizing the "instruments" of the mind.

Let us take a closer look at each of these principles.

Children need to be supported as they develop their ability to focus attention.

Vygotsky's ideas about a "zone of proximal development" (1980)—that a child needs the help of a more capable peer or teacher to master new challenges—have been long established in educational thinking. This view also applies to the early development of attention. Research shows that, from infancy, children have to be enticed by their primary caregivers to become engaged and focus attention (Greenspan & Shanker, 2004). Provided that the activities offered are engaging, this is accomplished most effectively through friendly eye-to-eye contact, touch, and vocalization (Messer, 1994; Tronick, 1989).

This encouragement and support of attention by early caregivers is done unconsciously for the most part. In the case of language-skills development, for example, Bruner (1985) describes how a caregiver responds to what a child is thinking and trying to communicate by deliberately repeating, recasting, or expanding on the child's utterance. What the caregiver probably does not realize is that more than language is being learned in such a process: the child's ability to focus attention is also being enhanced. According to Bruner—as well as developmental psychologists and linguists such as Shanker and Taylor (2001)—this process results in the child becoming an increasingly attentive and intentional participant in his or her environment.

"…an essential feature of learning is that it creates the zone of proximal development: that is, learning awakens a variety of internal developmental processes that are able to operate only when the child is interacting with people in his environment and in cooperation with his peers."

— Vygotsky, 1980, p. 89

Ways to Engage Children's Attention

©P

Instructional scaffolding is very closely related to all this, and it has had a major impact on educational practice. As a teacher, you know the importance of helping students with problems they find difficult, of planning hints or problem-solving cues for a difficult topic, and, when appropriate, of the benefits of peer-to-peer teaching and, for some students, computer-assisted learning. At its best, this kind of scaffolding teaches students the skills they need for learning *and* enhances their desire to learn. Before they can get to this point, however, their ability to focus attention needs to be developed, and scaffolding is integral to that process as well (Bandura, 1977; Vygotsky, 1980).

Focusing attention is taxing, and more so for some children than others. One of the oldest laws in psychology is the Yerkes-Dodson law, which is an inverted U-shaped curve showing the relationship between levels of energy and performance (Yerkes & Dodson, 1908). In simple terms, the Yerkes-Dodson law states that, while learning performance and the attention that it requires both demand energy, there is an optimal point in that performance. Beyond that point, continuing to expend energy undercuts sustained attention and can, in fact, bring on anxiety (see Figure 3.1).

Figure 3.1: Yerkes-Dodson Law

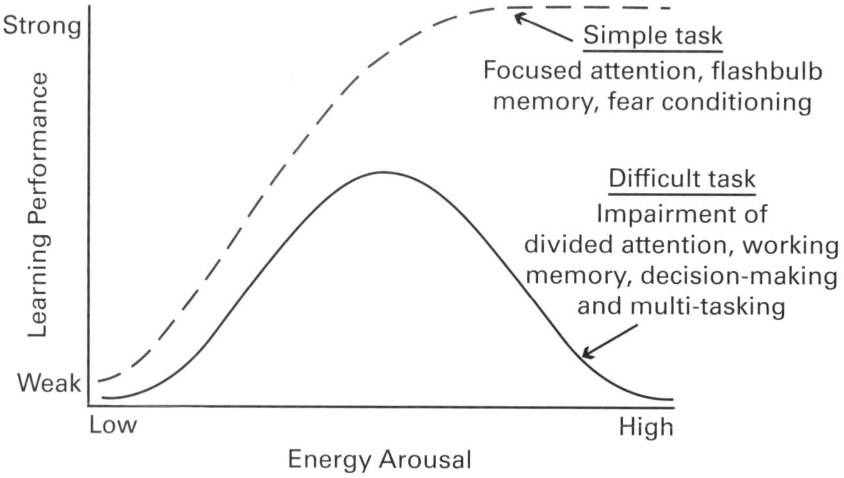

The Yerkes-Dodson Law, formulated in 1908, shows the relationship between levels of energy arousal and learning performance. The findings show that high levels of arousal can enhance the performance of simple learning tasks, but impair the performance of more complex tasks.

Schmeichel and Baumeister (2004) also demonstrated in a number of experiments how sustained attention can significantly deplete energy reserves, and how the ability to focus attention declines as a direct result of such energy expenditure. Porges (2011) argues that sustained attention has to be viewed within the entire context of the demands on a child. He has shown that during sustained attention there is a marked reduction of motor activity and a drop in heart-rate variability. In other words, the heart works with fewer "recovery" fluctuations and at an accelerated rate in order to meet the demands created by intense concentration.

Obviously the more engaging the work is, the more likely it is that students will remain focused and engaged in the task at hand. However, the fact is that focusing attention over a long period of time will drain a student's energy, diminishing his or her ability to sustain attention. A student's temperament may also affect his or her ability to stay engaged, and if there are other factors (physical, emotional, or social) also draining energy, it becomes even harder for that student to continue to focus.

Focusing attention requires fine-tuning and harmonizing the "instruments" of the mind.

In some ways, a teacher can be compared to the conductor of a school orchestra that starts out with the different instruments playing at different tempos and sometimes even different tunes. Our goal as a "teacher/conductor" is to guide a group of students who are disorganized at the start of the year to make music together by the end. Taking this analogy a step further, a teacher can be seen as the orchestra leader not just of the class as a whole, but of the mind of each individual student. In other words, a student with attention problems is like a fledgling musician who is constantly distracted by an itch, a sound, or a fly on his score, or one who constantly misses his cues because he is daydreaming. This comparison helps us to frame a number of critical questions:

- Why might different "instruments," or sections, in the student's mind be "out of tune" or not playing well together?

- What can we do to strengthen individual sections and promote the integration of all sections?

"A program of laboratory studies suggests that self-control depends on a limited resource, akin to energy or strength. Acts of self-control and, more generally, of choice and volition deplete this resource, thereby impairing the self's ability to function."
— **Baumeister, 2002, p. 129**

Auditory Processing—the ability to distinguish between similar sounds and words, separate speech from background noise, and recall and comprehend what was heard

"…thinking—as well as becoming a better thinker—isn't primarily about learning facts. It's about mastering senses, movement, and emotions."

— Greenspan & Greenspan, 2010, p. 74

Games to Enhance Auditory Discrimination

"There are two ways to think about attention. One way is to simply consider it a feature of the human nervous system. Either you can pay attention or you can't…. The other way to think about attention is that it is a learned process that develops gradually."

— Greenspan & Greenspan, 2010, p. 84

Learning to Focus Attention

• Why is this mental synchrony so critical for being able to remain calmly focused and alert? Conversely, why is mental asynchrony so disruptive and draining?

Stanley and Nancy Greenspan address such questions in their important book *The Learning Tree: Overcoming Learning Disabilities from the Ground Up* (2010). They tell the story of Sally, a Grade 3 student who was having trouble when asked to read in class. It soon became apparent that the source of Sally's problems lay in her **auditory processing**, a problem estimated to affect about 5 percent of school-aged children (KidsHealth, n.d.). While there was nothing wrong with her hearing as such, Sally had trouble processing what she heard because her brain and her ears were not working together. For example, it was difficult for her to differentiate between the words *bat* and *pat*, or to hear inflectional endings like *-ing* and *-ed*. And because it was hard for her to discriminate sounds, it was difficult for her to hold several sounds in her memory, so she had trouble reading multi-syllabic words properly. (Just imagine how hard it would be for you to memorize word lists in a language you did not speak, one with a radically different phonemic system than English.) As a result of the problems in her auditory processing, Sally's attention became very unfocused whenever she had to read.

Problems in her auditory processing also affected Sally's social development, because she had difficulty picking up subtle affect cues in different tones of voice, especially in a noisy schoolyard. Consequently, she had trouble understanding other people's intentions— were they teasing her or just being friendly? The school remedial reading program that Sally was involved in led to some improvement, but it was not until Stanley Greenspan began to work on the *root* causes of her particular learning problems that her reading (and social development) really improved. Greenspan's work included

• making Sally more aware of the nature of her auditory difficulties and the anxiety it was causing her

• asking her to play games that enhanced her auditory discrimination (e.g., Tone-A-Matic and Bear Wear)

• helping Sally to diminish sensory overload in her environment (e.g., teaching Sally to distance herself from noisy environments when she started to feel overwhelmed)

©P

Multimodal Adaptive Technologies

Multimodal Adaptive Technologies

Fast ForWord is an auditory training program designed for children who have an auditory processing disorder (APD). It is delivered via the internet and adapts to the user's level, offering challenges that match the user's ability to process auditory information. In turn, this enhances the user's ability to read, write, spell, and speak. The program is very intense—participants are expected to work for 100 minutes a day, five days per week. Published by Scientific Learning Corporation, there are now a number of programs offered under the brand name Fast ForWord that help students who experience challenges in reading.

Proloquo2Go™ is an excellent example of how technology can enable individuals who have expressive language disorders. The program comprises 14 000 symbols that users can tap to communicate their thoughts. Once tapped the program provides natural sounding text-to-speech voices. In addition, it can perform conjugations, predict words, and support multiple users. Proloquo2Go can be used by a broad range of users—from people who are just beginning to communicate to those who are fully literate but have lost their ability to speak. The technology is available to iPod, iPhone, and iPad users.

In another instance, Greenspan worked on the root causes of the attention problem of a Grade 2 child who had been clinically diagnosed as having **Attention Deficit Hyperactivity Disorder (ADHD)**. Greenspan at first spoke to the child in his normal tone of voice, asking all sorts of questions designed to elicit the child's interest, but he did not get a response. The child remained glued to a portable game console, his attention fixated on the intense visual and auditory stimuli provided by the game. How could Greenspan compete with this to get the child's attention?

After several minutes using his normal tone of voice, Greenspan suddenly increased the intensity and tempo of his voice. Essentially, he was trying to capture the boy's interest by matching the auditory stimulation provided by the game. The effect on the child was dramatic. Almost immediately, the boy put aside the console and

Attention Deficit Hyperactivity Disorder (ADHD)—a chronic condition affecting 7 to 12 percent of children. It includes a combination of problems, e.g., difficulty sustaining attention, hyperactivity, and impulsive behaviour. Children with ADHD often struggle with self-esteem, relationships, and performance in school. (ADD, an older term, describes children who are not hyperactive but have difficulty focusing.)

became engaged in a lengthy animated conversation about his favourite Pokémon game. Greenspan continued to ask questions that encouraged the boy to describe and compare Pokémon characters and their behaviour. The boy clearly enjoyed chatting with a friendly adult about this virtual world that, just a short time before, had completely absorbed his attention. At the same time, Greenspan had caught and kept the boy's attention precisely by making the play world of Pokémon the basis of their engagement.

Attention Deficit Hyperactivity Disorder

Head-Toes-Knees-Shoulders Game

"Beyond demographic variables or teacher's expectations, we found that the children in all the countries who performed well on the [Head-Toes-Knees-Shoulders] task did significantly better in math, vocabulary and early literacy."

— **McClelland, in Oregon State University, 2011, para. 7**

Games to Enhance Attention Regulation

SPOTLIGHT

Impulse-Control Games and Learning

A fascinating study by Shannon Wanless and Megan McClelland and their colleagues (Oregon State University, 2011) compares child-rearing practices in four countries (the United States, Taiwan, South Korea, and China). The study concludes that preschool children trained in Head-Toes-Knees-Shoulders, an impulse-control game similar to Simon Says, have enhanced attention regulation when they enter Grade 1 and, as a result, do significantly better in their formal schooling. (In the Head-Toes-Knees-Shoulders game, when the leader names a body part, the players are to touch a *different* body part. For instance, the children may be told that, when the leader says "head," they are to touch their knees.) Wanless has been careful to stress that the key to the success of the game is that it is fun.

Applications in the Classroom

Scenario

One day at a conference, I had a chat with Sherry, a Grade 3 teacher. Sherry had been teaching for 15 years. She had a number of students who had attention challenges, some more severe than others, but all at a level that impacted their learning and their participation in class. In the most severe instances, these students had trouble focusing during play activities.

©P

My first suggestion was for Sherry to read the curriculum and pedagogy presented in her province's early learning documents. Although these documents focus on younger children, much is applicable to all elementary school children. Grounded in play-based learning, in which Sherry was a firm believer, the documents promote the process of children working independently and gradually taking responsibility for their own learning.

I heard from Sherry several weeks later, and she still sounded frazzled. She had read the documents twice, but was continuing to have problems in her classroom. Asked to be specific about the nature of these problems, Sherry listed them as follows:

- Some students shy away from getting involved in any sort of activity, play or otherwise.

- Some students participate for a short time and then withdraw—and their peers do not understand this behaviour.

- Some students become hyperexcited when working or playing with others to the point that she has to step in to stem the excitement level.

- Without her constant presence, several students cannot follow even simple procedures.

What could I do or suggest now to help Sherry? I thought it would be instructive for her to first watch a video.

Making Learning Fun

The video I suggested that Sherry watch, which was filmed in a clinical setting, begins by showing a four-year-old boy wandering aimlessly around a room. Suddenly, he becomes fascinated as Chris, an occupational therapist, starts counting, "One, two, three,…" Within seconds, the boy begins to play a counting game with Chris and his mother, and becomes totally absorbed for a considerable length of time. While it looks quite spontaneous, this did not happen by accident. Chris had put a lot of thought into figuring out why the boy was having so much trouble engaging. It turns out the boy was having problems with his motor skills, and with integrating auditory and visual stimuli, all of which was making it virtually impossible for him

"Play is a vehicle for learning and lies at the core of innovation and creativity. It provides opportunities for learning in a context in which children are at their most receptive. Play and academic work are not distinct categories for young children, and learning and doing are also inextricably linked for them."
— **Pascal, 2009, para. 21**

to pay attention. Overall, Chris makes the whole game such fun that the joy the boy feels in playing it motivates him to overcome his challenges and start counting out loud himself. Very soon, he is the one who is trying to get Chris and his mother to keep playing!

Sherry was intrigued by the video. While the actions were more therapeutic than what she would do in her classroom, what struck her was the careful thought that had gone beforehand into what appeared to be such a spontaneous event. It inspired her to think of new ways to engage her students to help them learn how to become and remain focused in a classroom environment.

Games That Can Enhance Attention

As just noted, Sherry believed in the power of play to facilitate learning, so she did not need to be convinced of that. What she *did* need to become more aware of was the specific attention-getting and attention-keeping features of particular games as they relate to learning. Although Sherry knew that play-based learning is much more than playing games, she wanted to better understand why some games are so effective at enhancing children's attention.

Treasure Hunts, Orienteering, and Jigsaw Puzzles

Online Games for Children with Poor Visual-Spatial Processing

In her research, Sherry found that different kinds of games can be used to develop those aspects of a child's "mental team" that might need a bit more strengthening. For example, treasure hunts, orienteering, and jigsaw puzzles are often recommended for children with poor visual-spatial processing. Poor visual-spatial processing can mean, among other things, that a child has difficulties seeing or remembering visual patterns. Sherry concluded that the three activities identified above may help children with such problems by getting them to do one or more of the following:

- navigate their way through space

- coordinate written instructions with movements through space

- search for and recognize visual patterns

Sherry found that the fun offered by activities such as treasure hunts, orienteering, and puzzles could be used to help her students focus on clues that she could tailor to individual abilities. For example, the clues in a treasure hunt could be to walk a number of steps and then turn to the right or the left to look for a certain symbol that is partially hidden, or to solve a riddle. And with jigsaw puzzles, varying the number and size of pieces in a puzzle could provide a convenient way of adapting a game to match a student's abilities.

Obstacle Courses
An obstacle course in the classroom involves using objects such as desks, chairs, and plastic tunnels or large empty boxes as "obstacles" for children to crawl under, over, through, or otherwise get around. (Or, if those are not available, a "follow the leader" game in which students follow a sequence of actions done by a leader can be substituted.) Sherry found that obstacle courses were especially helpful for students who needed to strengthen their poor motor-coordination, which, as Greenspan (2009) has observed (see "Greenspan's Findings...," below), often lies at the heart of downstream attention difficulties. (Note that diagnosing of motor-coordination or similar problems should always be done by a specialist.)

"Sensory processing and motor abilities influence a child's emotional and cognitive development....they also affect a child's ability to attend and focus."
— **Greenspan, 2009, p. 161**

SPOTLIGHT

Greenspan's Findings on the Inability to Sequence Thoughts and Attention

Greenspan showed that an inability to sequence thoughts is often the source of a child's difficulties with attention. For example, if there are three steps that a child has to perform to solve a problem, and he gets lost at the second or third step, then his attention wanders. Greenspan discovered that, rather than trying to repeatedly drill the child in following the three steps, it was more effective to work on his ability to sequence his actions. Revealingly, Greenspan found that the better the child could execute three steps in a *motor* sequence (such as *hop, jump, clap*), the better he became at executing three steps in solving a problem.

The beauty of an obstacle course is that it can be tailored to suit the particular needs of individual children. It is also easy to scaffold by adding steps to increase the challenge, or by introducing elements to help the children work on impulse-control. Sherry started to use an obstacle course with her class that introduced two different kinds of sounds: a whistle and a bell. When the children running the course heard the whistle, they had to move as quickly as they could; when they heard the bell, they had to stand perfectly still until the bell sounded again. An additional benefit of offering an obstacle course was that, instead of competing against others, Sherry's students could compete against themselves to try to beat their own personal "records."

Based on her experiences with using obstacle courses, Sherry began experimenting with building movement components into core learning activities as well. For example, she found it highly effective when her students' attention began to wane to have them read and then imitate an animal whose name appeared on the interactive board. By varying the kinds of animals (e.g., "elephant" followed by "ant," "lion" followed by "snake"), she not only used movement to enhance their attention, but, by varying the types of animals and movements, also helped them learn how to modulate their own behaviours. When they were an elephant, they had to be very large and loud, but when they were an ant, they had to become very small and quiet.

Simon Says

Simon Says is a popular game that encourages the following:

- careful listening for the action called for (for example, "Simon says, 'Put your arms above your head'")

- impulse control (by resisting performing the action unless it is prefaced by "Simon says")

- observation (by watching carefully what the leader of the game does)

- imitation and execution of complex motor sequences (for example, hopping on one leg and then the other as the leader does)

- optimal emotion regulation as the game gets more exciting (that is, by staying calmly focused)

©P

Sherry was familiar with the game, but initially had found that several of her students could not play it without becoming angry or sullen. If she were to insist they play, that would take away the fun. Should she have daily Simon Says sessions until the students had mastered the skills? She reasoned that would not work either, for the students who found the game too taxing would soon refuse to participate, and the others would soon become bored.

With enjoyment as a given for all, Sherry found some methods to entice all to play and to increase enjoyment. The act of simplifying instructions or slowing down the pace of the game meant that all of her students could enjoy playing. Another adaptation that Sherry made was to divide the class into two groups to play, as suggested in Rae Pica's book *Great Games for Young Children* (2006, p. 39). Then, if a child moved without Simon's permission, he or she would move over to the other group and continue to play instead of being called "out" and confined to the sidelines.

Digital Games

Sherry asked about the potential benefits of introducing technology into her classroom as a means to strengthen attention. She knew that, as 21st-century learners, her students were fascinated with technology, but she wondered about the potentially negative effects of digital games. Could they become too absorbing for some children? Might some digital games overstimulate other children, thereby draining the energy they needed for optimal learning performance? After researching the pros and cons, Sherry decided that, if carefully managed and used for specific instructional purposes, digital games could be useful resources.

Interactive Dance Games

To start, Sherry introduced a video game console into her classroom for showing interactive dance games, such as DanceDance Revolution (2011) and Just Dance (2011). Games such as these gave her students a good physical workout and strengthened their attention while they were having fun. This was so successful on both fronts that Sherry occasionally used the console to show similar interactive programs on fitness and yoga.

Software That Can Enhance Attention

Encouraged by the impact of using digital games to enhance the attention of her students, Sherry also sought out software programs that could be used for educational purposes. One such program she learned about was FABtale (2009). FABtale can be used in the classroom to allow students to create their own multimodal versions of stories they are studying by combining text with video and audio resources from the internet. Classrooms in which such software has been tried have seen a dramatic increase in students' comprehension of the stories they were digitally reconstructing.

With older grades, FABtale can be used to create a virtual "newspaper." Students research and write columns on topics they find particularly interesting. They can merge text with video and music. This has proven to be an effective way of achieving personalized learning in a group activity, as well as a highly effective way of involving parents in students' school life.

FABtale

Criteria for Selecting Interactive Materials for the Classroom

Given the great number of interactive materials available, both for explicit educational purposes and otherwise, it is useful to have the following set of criteria to help select appropriate ones for the classroom.

It is suggested to choose interactive materials that

- encourage motor coordination and sequencing

- encourage body awareness, that is, individual consciousness of how the different parts of our bodies move in relation to each other and to the surrounding environment

- offer multimodal entry points

- encourage creativity (e.g., by enabling children to combine text, video, and music)

Developing Cognitive Self-Regulation

The emphasis up to this point has been on the sorts of things we can do as teachers to enhance our students' ability to focus attention. Of course, our ultimate goal in this chapter is the development of cognitive *self-regulation*. We want students to become aware of both

©P

the kinds of situations they find challenging and what they need to do to stay focused. With such a foundation, they will be much more capable of regulating their own learning. Figure 3.2 shows a cyclical model of self-regulated learning.

Figure 3.2: A Cyclical Model of Self-Regulated Learning

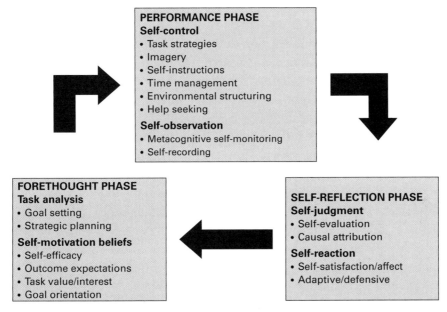

This model of self-regulated learning depicts its learning processes and motivational beliefs in three phases: forethought, performance, and self-reflection.

Source: Zimmerman & Campillo, 2002, p. 239

Self-regulated learners "approach educational tasks with confidence, diligence, and resourcefulness. Perhaps most importantly, self-regulated learners are aware when they know a fact or possess a skill and when they do not. Unlike their passive classmates, self-regulated students proactively seek out information when needed and take the necessary steps to master it."

— Zimmerman, 1990, p. 4

Drawing Up Some Rules

Inspired by her research on self-regulated learning, Sherry talked to her students about the classroom's rules, which, while in existence from the start of the year, had never been written down or consistently enforced. So, after Sherry wrote down a couple of rules of her own to start things off, the class engaged in a lengthy and lively discussion about what rules were needed and why. Sherry was pleased to hear her students coming up with carefully considered rules—and ramifications for not following them—involving such topics as respect for others, fair play, and ways to work collaboratively. When everyone agreed on the final list, it was printed and the "contract" was posted in the classroom for all to see. Weeks later, Sherry mentioned that her students were much more vigilant about following the rules than they had been when she alone had made them. Sherry was certain it was because the students had co-created the rules and therefore understood the rationale behind them.

Feeling Motivated

As Sherry read about self-regulated learning, she noticed how often "motivation" came up in the literature, particularly *intrinsic* motivation, which is being motivated to do something because it is enjoyable or interesting. She found research suggesting that the best teachers used any number of techniques, including but by no means limited to "cooperative learning techniques, holding individual students accountable for their learning, scaffolding student learning, making cross-curricular connections, encouraging student autonomy and choice, …making home–school connections, providing many opportunistic mini-lessons, making deep and personal connections to students, supporting appropriate risk-taking by students, making the classroom fun.…" (Brophy, Alleman, & Knighton, 2010, p. 11). Inspired, Sherry took advantage of every opportunity she could to more effectively motivate her students using these and other techniques, but frankly found it overwhelming.

Group Action

Because a number of students continued to experience difficulty working with their peers, with several becoming disengaged and disruptive even while playing games, Sherry had gradually reduced the amount of group activity her class was doing. Encouraged by research into how working in small groups can lead to more active involvement in learning (Good, Reys, Grouws, & Mulryan, 1989; O'Donnell & O'Kelly, 1994; Soli & Devine, 1976), Sherry decided to try again. She found that when the purpose of being in the group was clear to all, the students' behaviour in groups for both work and play was vastly improved. The class rules helped as well, with students often correcting others in their group for rule violations. And, because people take different roles when working in a group, and different roles can be given to different people at different times (Cohen, 1994; Johnson & Johnson, 2000), even the most underachieving students had their "turns in the spotlight." This confirms findings that students tend to help one another when they work in small groups; gifted students can deepen their learning by explaining concepts to others, and lower-achieving students benefit from the additional support offered by peers (Webb, 1991).

TJ: The Boy with the Sideways Cap
Always looking for more ideas to use in her class, Sherry eventually presented me with the case of TJ, the child who Sherry felt was having the most difficulty. Here is how she introduced his situation:

> The first day of classes, TJ slouched into the room. He wore baggy pants two sizes too large that were just barely hanging onto his hips, and a black T-shirt with a picture of a popular rapper on it, looking foreboding wearing dark sunglasses and holding up his fingers in a menacing gesture. I'd noticed TJ outside before class too, standing all alone, wearing a baseball cap that was turned sideways. Once in the classroom, TJ sprawled across his desk in a behaviour clearly meant to communicate that he was only there under duress. I started talking about seeing the rapper in a video on TV the night before, thinking that was something he might find interesting. But it was easy to see that TJ wasn't taking in a word that I was saying. He was only nine years old and yet already the light of learning that you would hope to see at this age wasn't there.

Sherry wondered what had led to this state and, more to the point, how she could change things for the better. The more we learn about early child development, the more we begin to understand that there is never a simple answer to such questions. This was certainly the case with TJ. His family lived in a pleasant neighbourhood, and his parents were both successful professionals who were deeply concerned about his future. They had tried to engage TJ in all sorts of activities, starting with sports and then moving to art and music, but he either refused to participate or would try an activity once or twice and then refuse to go back.

TJ's parents had confided in Sherry that his problems had started from birth. As a baby, he had difficulty falling asleep, he had problems feeding and learning how to walk, he was difficult to toilet-train, and he had trouble making friends. TJ's mother took him to organized activities for toddlers, but he would never join in. When asked what she thought the problem was, his mother answered that TJ was always restless and needed to constantly move about and feel things. He was also a little clumsy, which could explain why he did not like the various sports they had tried.

In daycare, TJ's behaviour became increasingly problematic. His parents enrolled him in an expensive facility with a beautiful outdoor space, but TJ soon resisted going. One day, the head of the daycare reported that TJ had refused to come back inside after playing outside, and became quite angry when he was forced to do so. His parents were told that TJ would not be allowed to stay unless they sought professional help for his behaviour.

TJ's parents took him to a therapist, who reported that the strongest emotion that she detected in their son was not anger. Instead, TJ's swagger, defiance, and frequent "tuning out" were strategies he used to protect himself from the *shame* he felt. The discovery: TJ lacked the sequencing abilities necessary to follow classroom activities, and he was worried that the important adults in his life would be angry with him for failing to understand.

Grades 1 and 2 were a struggle for TJ. He found it difficult to learn the alphabet and to follow stories. It was hard for him to stay on task but, paradoxically, once he did become engaged in a problem, he sometimes found it very difficult to disengage. And it remained as hard as ever for him to make friends. The years of being chastised were beginning to take their toll. By the time he reached Grade 3, TJ wasn't just subdued—he was unresponsive.

TJ's parents made arrangements for an occupational therapist to spend time with TJ after school to work on his motor skills. Rather than have him attempt sports that he might find too difficult, the therapist set up improvised obstacle courses, with tables he had to climb on top of, chairs he had to crawl under, a plastic tunnel he had to wriggle his way through, a mat for doing somersaults, a rope to climb up, and a trampoline at the end that he had to bounce across to reach the finish line.

TJ resisted at first, but by the time he reached the trampoline he was starting to be a nine-year-old again, begging for another turn. To make the obstacle course more interesting, the therapist gradually introduced all sorts of new challenges. There started to be subtle indications that it was working. Sherry noted that the morning slouch was beginning to disappear, and that TJ was even smiling a little when he came into class.

Sherry also found her attempts at introducing self-regulated learning in her class were having a positive effect on TJ. He was an eager participant when the class rules were being drawn up, passionately defending what he felt was "fair." And, after initially being a little withdrawn, he started to enjoy group work, especially when his talents in mathematics made him a popular "tutor" of others in the class. Sherry also found that TJ was beginning to listen more attentively to what was being expected of him, and he had started to join in on games during gym class. His classmates could sense that something was changing as well, and a few started asking TJ to come play with them during recess.

All this is not to say that TJ suddenly became a model of attentiveness. He still lapsed into long periods of daydreaming in some classes, and would come up with a dozen reasons why he could not work on reading his chapter books. However, there were definitely signs that TJ was improving.

Naturally enough, Sherry could not wait to share her excitement with TJ's parents. However, on parent night, before Sherry had a chance to share news about TJ's progress with his parents, his mother exclaimed, "TJ is a real handful, isn't he?" And the more enthusiastic Sherry became about how TJ was doing, the more his parents seemed to discount what she was saying. Sherry realized only after the meeting that perhaps the TJ she saw in her class was not the same child that his parents were seeing at home.

Tuning out had become a chronic mode of self-regulating for TJ early on. It was not just how TJ would respond to novel situations, but it was also how his parents, his teachers, and even his peers would respond to his general lack of response. Through their looks, gestures, and other affect signals, TJ's parents conveyed that they *expected* to be disappointed in him. Therefore, just telling TJ's parents about his transformation was not nearly powerful enough to dislodge them from their own expectations. They had to experience for themselves the changes that TJ was going through, as well as understand the kinds of subtle differences in their own behaviours that would assist him in this transition. It was critical for his parents to become a part of, help build on, and consolidate the changes that were starting to emerge in class.

Working with TJ's Parents

Sherry's first opportunity to engage the parents arose when TJ had to prepare a presentation for speech night. Sherry asked TJ's mother whether she could come after school to help him, and she agreed. When TJ and his mother sat together, however, the mother started to prompt TJ about what to write, at which point he got up from the table and walked to the windows. A look of frustration mixed with anger and embarrassment flashed across the mother's face. Before the mother could say anything, Sherry got up and joined TJ at the window. As the two stood there, Sherry wondered whether TJ was indicating what he wanted to write about, for he was staring intently at a mourning dove perched in a nearby tree. When Sherry asked him whether he would like to talk about birds in his speech, TJ became quite animated. TJ's mother told Sherry how much he loved birds, and the large number of birds he could identify by sight and even by call. Was this the same boy who had been diagnosed earlier as having trouble discriminating musical notes?

As his mother talked, TJ seemed to swell with pride. He returned to the table, sat down, picked up the pencil, and began to say aloud and write his speech, which—no surprise!—was about birds. Without any prompting, TJ filled an entire page. He wrote about the birds that lived in his backyard—what they looked like and how they behaved. When he finished, his mother suggested, "Why don't you tell them about the robin that built a nest on the deck outside your bedroom last spring?" TJ added that detail, but when his mother suggested that he tell the class about the baby chicks as well, TJ shook his head, indicating that his speech was done. He proceeded to read the entire speech aloud and then, pleased with the result, went off to find one of his friends.

©P

Working with Parents

For parents inquiring about ways to help their child work with his or her strengths and weaknesses, you might suggest that they

Helping Children Understand Their Strengths and Weaknesses

- help their child to develop and preserve optimism that he or she can and will be successful

- never put their child down or compare him or her unfavourably to others, but instead focus on their child's strengths and nurture the idea that everyone has something valuable to offer

- encourage their child to be accountable for the responsibilities he or she takes on, and share their pride when they act responsibly

- let you know that they are interested in working with you and other school staff members to strengthen those areas in which their child requires some extra help

TJ's mother later remarked that she had lost count of how many times she had been told that TJ's problem was that he would not apply himself. That was not what happened here. Rather, the lesson learned was that when TJ was given the chance to choose a topic he found interesting, and one in which he could take the lead, he was able to overcome the anxiety that made it so difficult for him to sequence and express his thoughts. Moreover, TJ's mother enjoyed the experience as much as he did, and she conveyed this with smiles and encouraging comments. By contrast, imagine what would have happened if TJ had been instructed to write one page on a topic that he could not relate to, and his mother's role had been to act as a disciplinarian. TJ very likely would have rebelled against the task and, if forced, would have done a lacklustre job for the sake of getting it done.

This success suggests a new way of approaching one of the most unpopular of practices—homework. Consider getting parents more involved in this area. Asking parents to do so can improve communication between home and school because you get the opportunity to clarify for parents what is expected of their child while giving them an idea of what their child is learning. You may even have the opportunity to get them to serve as important agents in developing their children's ability to focus attention.

Where appropriate, parents can

- help their child with time management (e.g., help their child commit to a set time for doing homework and plan for how long they think a task will take)

- model self-regulation (e.g., do their own "homework," such as pay bills or catch up with reading, while the child is doing his or her homework)

Breaking a Homework Task into Chunks

- discuss with their child what work he or she finds the easiest and the hardest to do—a metacognitive task—and then encourage him or her to do the most difficult task or subject first

TJ: The Boy with the Cap on *Straight*

Later, when asked for one or two highlights of her dealings with TJ, Sherry first identified something to do with herself: "For me, it was when I realized that, for a child who was so susceptible to being ashamed of his weaknesses, the worst thing I could do was to embarrass him still further for his behaviour in class, or to set up challenges for him that he would not be able to meet." Then she laughed and added, "And the second was the moment I was convinced that TJ himself had turned the corner—the day I saw him walking to school with his baseball cap on *straight!*"

The more I thought about this, the more I wondered whether TJ had not simply found the perfect metaphor to show the world what he was feeling—for he himself had been askew, the one who always felt ashamed and uncomfortable. There was something so poignant about his choice of a 1970s gang symbol from the Chicago housing projects whose meaning he could only dimly understand. Yet the way he had worn his cap was so full of meaning. He wanted the world to know how unhappy he was, how much he wanted help. Fortunately, TJ's cry was heard and, as his newly positioned cap told us, he was now headed in a new direction.

©P

Enhancing Students' Ability to Pay Attention

- Issues with cognition could have a physical basis. So, if they have not already done so, encourage parents to have their child's hearing and vision checked. If both are fine, and a student continues to have difficulty understanding directions or sequenced instructions, for example, a speech-language therapist may need to be consulted.

- Use teaching and learning techniques consistently so students know what to expect and can focus accordingly.

- Watch for opportunities throughout the day to offer instructional scaffolding to students who are having trouble focusing attention. For example, provide additional help in the form of hints, links, and cues to a student, then gradually withdraw the assistance as it is no longer required.

- Students with auditory processing problems have trouble under-standing and following directions, which is often mistaken for not focusing attention. There are a number of tips you can use with these students:

  - Break down instructions into simpler, smaller steps.
  - Provide instructions in more than one mode (oral, written).
  - Ensure the student is looking at you when you speak, if possible.
  - Ask the student to repeat what you have said.
  - Seat the student in a place where he or she has a clear sightline to you during instructional time.

- Provide students with a quiet place where they can retreat to if they start to feel overwhelmed by distractions in their environment.

- Look for ways to make learning fun. Games such as the following are both fun and can help develop self-regulation in the cognitive domain:

  - Statues, Red Light/Green Light, and Musical Chairs (require children to listen, move, and stop on cue)

– Simon Says (requires children to remember and think before they act; the challenge of the game can be increased for older children by calling out multiple steps, such as: "Simon Says hop on your right foot, turn around once, put your right hand on your left ear, and then clap your hands twice.")

– There are also many free digital versions of memory games available online.

Online Memory Games

- Deliver complex instructions in more than one mode (e.g., discuss the instructions with the students and together create a list that is posted for all students).

Developing Cognitive Self-Regulation

- Help students to become aware of the kinds of situations they find challenging and what they need to do to stay focused.

- Provide students with collaborative learning experiences to encourage social self-regulation as students help one another as they work in small groups. For more on collaborative learning, see Chapter 4 (pp. 80–81).

- Be sensitive to students' actions. A student who appears bored may in fact be intimidated by a challenging activity. If you feel that is the case, try lowering the level of difficulty until students start to show success at handling the challenge presented. (On the other hand, do not make the task too easy, as that also will cause boredom.)

- As appropriate, allow students to select their own activities and set their own goals. Autonomy can play an important part in the development of self-regulation.

- Help students with problems in the cognitive domain to recognize that there are things they can do when they start to feel overwhelmed or left behind, such as start to listen more closely or ask questions about things they are unsure of.

- Encourage students with auditory processing problems to write about topics they are interested in. For older students, the use of organizers such as flow charts or mind maps will prove useful in helping them to remember important ideas.

©P

Chapter 4

The Social Domain

Key Attributes of the Social Domain

Children who are optimally self-regulated in the social domain will have the ability to

- understand their feelings and intentions

- understand the feelings and intentions of others

- respond to the feelings and intentions of others appropriately, both verbally and nonverbally

- monitor the effects of their responses on others

- be an effective communicator—as a listener and as a speaker

- demonstrate a good sense of humour that does not rely on ridicule

- recover from and repair breakdowns in interactions with others (e.g., through compromise)

Our daily interactions with others take place in the social domain, in the many and varied circumstances in which we chat, exchange ideas, become involved in recreational activities, collaborate on projects, do volunteer or charity work, and so on. In this chapter, we will look closely at self-regulation in the social domain, especially in school settings.

School is the ultimate social world that a child must learn to deal with, complete with its own complex set of rules for appropriate behaviour both in the classroom and on the playground. Children struggling to self-regulate at the physiological and emotional levels can find the social domain extremely stressful, and conversely, problems in the social domain can exacerbate self-regulatory problems at all the other levels of our five-domain model.

Many highly effective social and emotional learning (SEL) programs have been established to help children master the various skills needed to flourish in the social domain. In this chapter, we will review why such programs are so beneficial for reducing social stress. In particular, the goals of this chapter are

1. to see why SEL programs play a critical role in an overall self-regulation strategy

2. to see how situating SEL programs within the framework of self-regulation (e.g., understanding the importance of biological and emotional difficulties) will enhance the effectiveness of these programs

What Is Social Intelligence?

What Is Social Intelligence and Why Is It Important?

We cannot look at social self-regulation without exploring the concept of social intelligence. A number of psychologists identify social intelligence as a set of distinct emotional, "mind reading," and communication skills that a child must master in order to flourish socially (Bar-On, 2005; Gardner, 1983; Goleman, 2006; Jones & Day, 1997). These skills are summarized in Figure 4.1.

©P

Figure 4.1: The Skills of Social Intelligence

Emotional Skills	• understand what emotions are considered appropriate in certain situations (e.g., sadness at a funeral, happiness at a wedding) • modulate emotional responses (e.g., not get overly excited, not become too subdued) • understand more complex human emotions, such as trust, envy, and resentment
"Mind Reading" Skills	• recognize that others have their own thoughts, beliefs, feelings, and desires • understand how someone else views a situation • understand the effect of what we say or do on someone else
Communication Skills	• learn subtle "languacultural" conventions (Shanker, 2001) • understand the value of taking turns in exchanges • pay attention to the importance of context in communication situations (e.g., not speak too loudly when expressing an idea in a small group; shout to warn someone not to cross a street because of an oncoming car) • know how to repair communication breakdowns • learn that statements made have implications for behaviour (e.g., that saying "I'm sorry" after hitting someone is not enough; saying so should also strongly imply that "I will not hit you again")

Emotional-Social Intelligence (ESI)

"The ingredients of social intelligence I propose here can be organized into two broad categories: social awareness, what we sense about others— and social facility, what we then do with that awareness."

— **Daniel Goleman, 2006, p. 84**

Ways to Support Children's Communication Skills

It is important to recognize the self-regulation roots of these social intelligence skills. Children who have difficulty with self-regulation often find it very difficult, if not impossible, to develop and exercise social skills (Casenhiser, Shanker, & Stieben, 2011). For these children, social situations are likely to worsen their self-regulation problems in other domains. For example, if a child becomes very anxious in groups, she may become hypoactive and try to withdraw from them or, on the other hand, become hyperactive and find it very difficult to learn participatory skills such as turn-taking in discussions and play situations. No doubt, you can think of children in your classroom who exhibit such behaviour.

Co-regulation—a process in which two individuals observe and understand each other and adjust their behaviour to help each other reach optimal levels of regulation

Fortunately, you can probably also think of children who demonstrate the opposite. These are the children in your class who are optimally self-regulated, and who do very well in both their social relationships and their academic work. These children can be said to have high social intelligence. Such children, it is also important to recognize, are very good at **co-regulation**.

The Co-Regulation "Dance"

Co-regulation is a process in which two individuals are socially "in sync" with each other because they

- understand what is on each other's mind by making sense of each other's affect cues and gestures (for example, the meaning of a grimace, the tone or volume of a voice, or a hand raised in greeting)

- recognize the effects of each person's behaviour on the other

- adjust their behaviour to help up-regulate or down-regulate each other as necessary

The Dance Metaphor

"The chief appeal of the dance metaphor is that it draws attention to how communicating partners continuously establish and sustain a feeling of shared rhythm and movement."

— Shanker & King, 2002, p. 606

Co-Regulation: How People Help Each Other Regulate

The above behaviours have been likened to an intricate "dance" in which two partners are constantly moving in and out of being in step with one another as they recognize and try to repair communication breakdowns (Shanker & King, 2002). Such a "dance," it is now recognized, actually begins very early as mothers and others interact with the infants under their care (see "The Cellphone Chronicles: The Beginnings of Co-Regulation").

It is hardly surprising that some children find co-regulation very challenging. It encompasses the demands of the social domain, which can be intensely stressful. The more hypo- or hyperaroused such children are, the more difficult and anxiety-causing it is for them to recognize, process, and react appropriately to the many fast-paced cues and responses that characterize social interactions at school, at home, and elsewhere (Goodwin, 1981). Studies have shown that simply slowing the pace of such cues and responses can help children who struggle in the social domain to make sense of them and become better at co-regulating (Gepner & Féron, 2009).

©P

The Cellphone Chronicles:
The Beginnings of Co-Regulation

One day at an Early Years Centre, I observed a mother happily engaged with her nine-month-old son in a game of touching different parts of each other's face. For example, the mother would smile and tap the baby's nose while saying, "That's your nose," and the baby would respond by giggling with a wide-eyed look, waiting for the next surprise. Suddenly the ringing of her cellphone distracted the mother, and the baby's efforts to recapture her attention were met with no success. When the mother re-engaged with her baby about two minutes later, the child suddenly leaned forward and tried to bite her on the arm. In a flash, the mother's facial expression and vocalizations became harsh. She angrily withdrew from the interaction, and the baby quickly responded by starting to cry. The mother was unaware of why their connection had broken down, and was genuinely surprised when a facilitator walked her through the interaction.

When the same baby was around 11 months old, a similar interaction started to unfold. This time, the cellphone rang just as the baby was trying to pull off his mother's glasses. On this occasion, though, the mother told the caller, "I'll have to call you back," and immediately returned her attention to her child. She responded to the baby's angry look by softly asking, "What's the matter?" before offering to pick him up and cuddle him. The baby reacted with a softening of his grimace and a look of expectation. The mother responded in turn by reaching closer to the baby, who now broke into a smile as he reached his hands toward her. A few seconds later, she was snuggling him and patting his back, and the baby looked visibly relaxed. Perhaps the most interesting part of all was when, now calmly cradled in his mother's arms, the baby reached forward once again to take his mother's glasses, and she chuckled as she let him take them off and peer through them.

In this situation, we can see how the baby's social development is strengthened by the way in which exchanges of affect signals between mother and child—a gentle tone of voice, a cuddle, a look of expectation, a smile, laughter—modulated an interaction that might easily have broken down. This example further demonstrates how, in this optimal state of social co-regulation in which child and mother are jointly and calmly focused, the baby is encouraged to continue his exploration of the world.

How Regulation, Self-Regulation, and Co-Regulation Are Linked

As a teacher, you will have seen behaviours like the following that involve up- and down-regulating:

- *Child A* tries to re-engage *Child B* in a schoolyard game after the latter withdraws in a sulk because of feelings of inadequacy.

- *Child C* gently puts a hand on the shoulder of *Child D*, who is anxiously looking out the classroom window with arms tightly folded.

- *Child E* gets *Child F* to laugh at a joke to distract and help the latter calm down when he gets upset because he cannot solve a math problem.

- *Child G* assists *Child H*, who is shy and has reading difficulties.

You have probably noted that Child A and Child G are involved in *up*-regulating their peers, while Child C and Child E are attempting to *down*-regulate theirs. At the root of what the four "helping" children are doing is their ability to connect with what their peers are feeling and to respond accordingly. Moreover, these four children have acquired these social-intelligence skills by themselves being regulated countless times—by parents, teachers, and others—and *internalizing* such regulation to become better at *self*-regulating. In turn, this makes them adept at helping to regulate their peers.

Now let us look at three more complicated social situations:

- *Child I* sees *Child J* crying because she is upset, and he teases her to try to distract her.

- *Child K* sees *Child L* crying because he is upset, and she pokes him to try to calm him down.

- *Child M* sees *Child N* struggling to get her mitts on and tries to help her, which infuriates Child N, in turn, angering Child M.

In the first situation above, Child I has good intentions but has not learned appropriate techniques for down-regulating Child J to help her feel better. Inappropriate attempts at down-regulating are also evident in the next situation. Here, Child K likely has poor motor control, which results in a poke, rather than a comforting pat. The third situation draws attention to the constant assessing and adjusting—reflective of social intelligence—required for optimal co-regulation: that is, the need to modify one's behaviour on the basis of understanding how someone else responds to it. In this case, Child M does not understand Child N's need for independence, cannot figure out why his attempt to help is making matters worse and, as a result, becomes dysregulated himself.

Helping Children Learn to Repair Communication/Social Breakdowns

Ultimately, for children to thrive as learners as well as in their general development as social beings, they need to *co*-regulate, not just regulate, each other. In general, the more two or more children "resonate" with each other emotionally, the better they co-regulate. And the better they co-regulate, the better a less experienced partner can learn from a more experienced one, the better two individuals can jointly problem solve and play happily together, and the better members of a group can function in classrooms and other social environments. Figure 4.2, on the next page, shows an overview of the connections between regulation, self-regulation, and co-regulation.

Figure 4.2: The Connections Between Regulation, Self-Regulation, and Co-Regulation

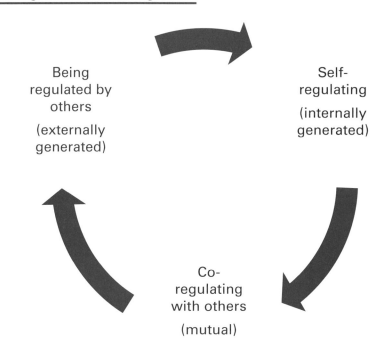

Tips for Co-Regulating with Your Children

21st Century Skills

Collaborative Learning Opportunities

In recent years, there has been increased focus on the skills that employers consider critical in new employees—the ability to problem solve, to think critically, to show initiative, and to collaborate with employees and clients are examples.

This shift of emphasis is evident in the plethora of 21st century skills foci—including those of organizations such as The Partnership for 21st Century Skills (2011) and documents such as "Competencies for 21st Century Learning" (Alberta Education, 2011). In 2010, the Ontario Ministry of Education released a brochure in advance of student progress reports that introduced learning skills and work habits that reflected some of these workplace demands, including responsibility, independent work, initiative, organization, collaboration, and self-regulation (York Region District School Board, 2010).

©P

While it is possible to look at two of these skills and habits independently—collaboration and self-regulation—they are mutually enhancing. Collaborative learning, with its focus on student-centred learning, shifts the locus of control from the teacher's hands to those of the student, thereby increasing student ownership and responsibility. The makeup of collaborative groups reflects the range of abilities found in any classroom. Boekaerts and Corno (2005, p. 220) believe that collaborative learning supports self-regulation: students who are lower achieving benefit from the opportunity to work with more able peers. Similarly, these more able students benefit because they have the opportunity to act as models.

These benefits of collaborative learning are in addition to those all students (and teachers) gain through pursuing learning opportunities that are engaging, that allow students to showcase strengths in different ways, and that allow them the opportunity to engage with peers on real learning tasks. There are a number of books that explore the benefits of collaborative learning—particularly good are Greene (2001, 2008) and Greene and Ablon (2005). With districts across the country committing to implementation of self-regulation strategies, it is likely that we will see more evidence of how collaborative learning and self-regulation benefit all students.

Applications in the Classroom

Scenario

Each of the earlier scenarios in this resource involved a single teacher working on the aspect of self-regulation that was the focus of that chapter. This time we will look not at a classroom, but at an entire school—in fact, at an entire community.

The community in question had been the victim of political and social neglect over many years. My first walk around the community was unsettling. Homes showed neglect, very few people were outside, and a field that had been intended as a community park was littered and desolate.

The major concerns of the teachers at the local elementary school came as no surprise: a lack of student engagement and a general lack of "connectedness" between the community and the school. The teachers themselves appeared to be very dedicated, but they were feeling burned out. As in many districts, every two or three years they had been required to implement a new educational initiative to manage the students' behaviour. In fact, the teachers had just spent the past year training on the latest offering, which had only partly addressed issues related to social self- and co-regulation. Understandably, then, they were concerned that I might be there to impose yet another pre-packaged program on them, one not customized to deal with their specific needs. Furthermore, it became clear that, as with so many such programs, the latest one that the teachers had tried emphasized children *being* regulated rather than *self-* and *co*-regulating. Essentially, this most recent program promoted the use of "command-and-control" behavioural management techniques to induce compliance (giving rewards for good behaviour and taking away rewards for "bad" behaviour). These behavioural management techniques included

- putting students into groups of four, and giving them a star for being quiet and taking one away for being noisy. When a group accumulated enough stars, it received a treat.

- a "management book" in which each student's day was divided into five sections to cover the five periods of the school day. In these sections, the teacher recorded check marks for "good" behaviour and Xs for "bad" behaviour. Each child's check marks were totalled at the end of the day, and a score of 24 or higher earned a reward.

- a "discipline mat" or time-out area for a student considered to be misbehaving

- a note sent home to parents, detailing their child's misbehaviour that day, which the parents had to sign

While such methods were useful for some of the students in some situations, they did little to enhance the children's social intelligence because there was little, if any, recognition of the crucial importance of self- and co-regulation in social interactions. Most important was the need to work on the underlying factors—the hyperarousal, emotional dysregulation, and underdeveloped social-intelligence skills. Very simply, fear of punishment alone would have done little to cultivate such skills, and may in some cases have actually impeded their development.

Tackling the Issues

In broad and practical terms, everyone—students, teachers, school administrators, and parents—needed to become engaged in the process of creating a successful program. To achieve this, we introduced a number of approaches beginning immediately with regular workshops on arousal, self-, and co-regulation for all grades in the school. These workshops would continue throughout the school year, as would our emotion and social regulation program.

Exercise and Diet

In Chapter 1, we discussed how overload in one of the two nervous systems (the sympathetic nervous system, SNS, and the parasympathetic nervous system, PNS) can cause the other system to overwork. This leads to children being either hyper- or hypoaroused. Since the underlying mechanisms of self-regulation ultimately reside in the biological domain, we must always take that domain into account when dealing with issues related to self-regulation. To start tackling the problems with social interaction in this elementary school, we had to begin by tackling children's difficulties with arousal regulation. Many of them had problems related to hyperarousal, with some experiencing symptoms that are typically associated with Attention Deficit Hyperactivity Disorder (ADHD).

Attention Deficit Hyperactivity Disorder

  As few of the students at the school were exercising sufficiently, eating a healthy diet, or getting enough sleep, many were chronically hypo- or hyperaroused. To address this problem, we started a breakfast club before school to provide students with low-glycemic foods (oatmeal, corn meal muffins, and fresh fruit) that would provide a lasting source of energy for the morning's work. Rather than describing this as a "breakfast club"—a term that, unfortunately, had acquired a negative connotation—we called it "Fit and Fuelled." The idea here, which turned out to be extremely popular, was to begin the school day with an exercise regimen (soccer for some, calisthenics and power yoga for others), followed by the "fuel" that these "young athletes" had earned and needed.

Workshops for Teachers

We also started a series of workshops on arousal, self-, and co-regulation for the teachers. In the workshops, we concentrated on helping the teachers to understand the causes of hypo- and hyper-arousal, and looked at strategies and techniques for up-regulating or down-regulating students both in and out of class—for example, decreasing the amount of time that students had to sit at their desks, changing their work environments so that they had an opportunity to work at different class centres and with different group compositions, and reducing noise levels and visual distractors (see Chapter 1, pp. 12–14).

One of the most fruitful workshops began with a discussion about recent research that showed that sustained anxiety exacerbates how much discomfort a child feels. For example, Schmidt, Richey, & Fitzpatrick (2006) developed the Discomfort Intolerance Scale (DIS), a five-item self-report instrument that examines how much one can tolerate uncomfortable physical sensations. Children who find certain kinds of stimuli difficult to handle—for example, loud noise, bright lights, or the noise and movement of other children—will experience a much greater physiological drain than a child without such vulnerabilities. Additionally, their heightened anxiety will intensify the painfulness of something as simple as bumping an elbow. In turn, this sets off a drain on their nervous system that significantly reduces their ability to inhibit impulsive behaviour.

One teacher mentioned a child in her JK class who was constantly bumping into things and then screaming in pain and begging for an ice pack. The teachers spent some time talking about this behaviour. Was the child seeking attention? Was giving the child the ice pack a way of reinforcing a need for attention? Was this a behaviour that could be traced back to how the child's caregivers had responded to such outbursts? Should the child simply be ignored? Of course, the overriding question that needed an answer was how to stop this behaviour.

Before dealing with the preceding questions, I asked the teachers to think about *why* the child might be asking for an ice pack. One teacher remarked that ice can relieve pain and have a very calming effect on the nervous system. This triggered a discussion about why the child might be so sensitive to pain, and why she was possibly down-regulating by using the ice packs. In other words, the request

©P

for ice packs could be a sign that this child was prone to hyper-arousal and was trying to deal with this. We then looked at why this particular child might be prone to hyperarousal. The teachers had two main answers: the child (a) was dealing with intense family stresses at home, and (b) found it difficult to cope with the hubbub of the class. This last reason could also explain her frequent requests to go to the bathroom—was she using this as an escape from the class? We agreed that, in addition to the ice packs, the child would benefit from having access to a quiet space in the classroom to help her down-regulate when necessary.

The point of this example is not to show that a problem like this can be solved in a relatively brief workshop discussion. Rather, it illustrates a very critical point:

> It is essential that we look at students through a different lens, to shift from thinking in terms of behaviour management to figuring out why we see certain behaviours and what can be done to help these students learn to self-regulate.

By the end of this particular workshop, the teachers had moved from thinking about how to stop the behaviour to focusing on two topics: (1) the causes of the behaviour, and (2) how they could mitigate the stressors on the child so that she never got to the point of crying out for ice packs.

Parenting Workshops
During the course of the year, we also held six parenting workshops, which were entirely voluntary and generally well attended. In the first, by way of an overview, we explained the nature of stress and its effects on a child's everyday behaviour and ability to self-regulate. In the remaining workshops, we looked at the importance of the following for children:

Parenting Workshops

- sleep and a regular sleep routine

- a healthy diet

- fulfilling free-time activities, including daily exercise

- limited exposure to television and video games

- appropriate discipline strategies

Music and Prosocial Behaviour

"This proclivity [to produce and to enjoy musical behaviours]… encouraged the children in our study to behave more cooperatively and pro-socially towards each other."

— **Kirschner & Tomasello, 2010, p. 363**

Online Vocabulary-Building Games

A School Choir

Early on in our social and emotional regulation program, a decision was made to form a school choir, which one of the teachers offered to direct. A choir made sense because not only did it involve minimal cost, there is also research showing that singing in a choir is highly effective for promoting social self-regulation in children (Kirschner & Tomasello, 2010). Membership in a choir requires participants to monitor themselves and one another, as well as move together in time and harmony to realize a shared goal. The choir sang at a number of school events throughout the year, and the performances attracted many of the parents and other members of the children's families.

Vocabulary-Building Word Games

Ever since Betty Hart and Todd Risley published *Meaningful Differences in the Everyday Experience of Young American Children* (1995), we have known that children from lower-income homes, such as the students at this school, are exposed to far fewer words than children from middle- and upper-income homes. Hart and Risley's research found that the average child in a lower-income home hears about 600 words an hour, while a child in a middle-income home hears about 1250 words, and a child in an upper-income home hears about 2150 words.

With this research in mind, and noticing the limited vocabulary of the children at this school, we introduced vocabulary-building sessions involving games that we adapted or created for our purposes. The overriding goal was to increase the frequency and scope of the children's vocabulary related to the emotions and "mind reading" so that they could improve their relationships with others. A favourite game was "Scatter Words," played as follows:

1. The teacher divided the class into teams of five, and asked each team to come up with 3 words for positive and/or negative emotions, based on their own experiences or on something they had recently seen or read.

2. The teacher wrote the words suggested by the teams on the board in two separate lists, one headed "Positive Emotions" and the other "Negative Emotions." (For the inevitable duplications, and to bring the total number of words up to at least 5 in each list, the teacher could add or substitute emotion words of her own.)

©P

3. Once there were at least 10 different words on the board, the teacher "scattered" their individual letters on the board.

4. Each team then had to come up with as many additional emotion-related words as they could using the individual letters—but without repeating any of the words already listed on the board. The team that came up with the most words was the winner.

Another activity that a Grade 1 teacher came up with that was usable in all grades was "What Is This Person Feeling?" It worked as follows:

1. The teacher put a photograph of someone on the board and asked students to come up with different words to characterize what they thought the person was feeling.

2. Suggested words were written on the board for everyone to see.

3. Several students were challenged to tell a brief story about how the person in the picture might be feeling, and why.

4. A natural extension of the game was to have students then use the basis of their story for dramatic play.

We noticed immediately that the students tended to overuse certain words or expressions, often very colloquial ones, in this and other word games. We suggested to the teachers that, rather than correct the students' initial word choice, we build on whatever the students stated to get an emotion-focused conversation going. Here is how one teacher handled the following fairly difficult situation that arose after she showed a student a photograph of a man who looked worried and sad.

> **Teacher:** "So, what do you think the man in the picture is feeling?"
>
> **Child:** "I think he's bummed out."
>
> **Teacher:** "Why do you think he's bummed out?"
>
> **Child:** "Well, I guess because today is the day the social worker comes to see him at his apartment, and she's going to tell him that he needs to find a job."
>
> **Teacher:** "So do you think he's feeling angry or sad?"

Child: "Yeah, a little of both."

Teacher: "And how do you think he feels about not having a job?"

Child: "I guess he wishes he had one."

Teacher: "Do you think it's possible to feel all these emotions at the same time: angry and sad and maybe even a little ashamed?"

Child: "Yeah."

Helping Children to Understand Others and How They Affect Others

Emotion Cards and Emotion-Related Activities

Once the children at all grades were (a) showing signs of improved arousal and emotion regulation, and (b) demonstrating evidence, through their expanding repertoire of words, of improved social intelligence in their ability to understand and talk about emotions, we decided to enrich the program with different "mind reading" sessions for the junior and senior grades.

"Mind-Reading" Activities: JK to Grade 3 Students
In this initiative, students were buddied up. Each partner was asked to describe how the other was feeling and to provide possible reasons. The students turned out to be very well aware of—and very clear in expressing—what the buddy was feeling, why the buddy was feeling that way, and what might make the buddy feel better. For example, a Grade 1 child, after observing a buddy who was very withdrawn, commented that he must be really sad because his cat was missing and worried that the animal might have been run over by a car. When the teacher asked the child how she might help her buddy become less sad, worried, and withdrawn, the child suggested lending her buddy one of her toys that she knew the child liked. Her suggestion worked!

The students enjoyed these sessions. To make things more interesting, the teacher regularly changed the pairings of buddies, offering the students opportunities to recognize and talk about different emotions in different people, as well as encouraging them to learn how to co-regulate with a wider circle of friends. It was no surprise that the students knew what their closest friends were feeling. The big surprise was how attuned they were to what most of the other students in the class were feeling as well.

                    ©P

S P O T L I G H T

Reaching In...Reaching Out (RIRO): Promoting Resilience in Young Children

Reaching In...Reaching Out (RIRO) resiliency skills training provides professionals who care for and work with children under the age of eight with the knowledge and skills they need to model and teach critical abilities associated with resilience. These critical abilities include

RIRO Resiliency Skills Training

- being in charge of our emotions
- empathizing with others
- analyzing the cause of problems
- reaching out to others and opportunities

"Mind-Reading" Activities: Grades 4 to 6 Students

In our everyday social interactions, we commonly figure out what other people are thinking or feeling from the expressions on their faces, their tones of voice, and their gestures. To help these older students become better at interpreting such a wide range of cues, thereby exercising their social intelligence, the teacher had them imagine that they were going to ask their parents for a special treat (for example, permission to sleep over at a friend's house or some money for a treat). The teacher posed this question: "Would you ask your parents for this treat if you saw that they were in a bad mood, or would you wait until you saw that they were in a good mood?" All of the students agreed that they would wait until their parents were in a good mood. Now the teacher asked them to prepare a list of things that would tell them when their mother or father was in a good mood and when they were in a bad mood. To help them, they were instructed to create and complete the chart shown in Figure 4.3 (see the next page).

Figure 4.3: Body Language Identification Chart

Cues	Description	What the behaviour indicates the person is feeling, and why I think so
Facial expressions		
Tone of voice		
Gestures		
Body posture		
Body movements		
Other (describe)		

The students then played a game that demonstrated how much we use other people's body language to figure out what is going on in their minds. Half the class watched a half-hour drama with the volume turned off, while the other half watched it with the sound on. Each group used its chart to record what they thought the main characters were feeling, and then the two groups compared notes. The groups were astonished to find how similar the two charts were. In other words, even though half the class had not heard a single word of the drama, they did quite well identifying what was going on in the story and in the minds of the major characters, just by reading the affect cues of the characters.

SPOTLIGHT

PATHS Program

PATHS (Promoting Alternative THinking Strategies) Program

The PATHS program is an elementary school social and emotional learning curriculum that helps children handle emotions positively, empathize, make responsible decisions, and resolve conflicts peacefully. The program has three major units: (1) Self-Control, (2) Feelings and Relationships, and (3) Interpersonal Cognitive Problem Solving. The unit on feelings and relationships focuses on emotional and interpersonal understanding, with learning activities that teach children the cues for self-recognition of their own feelings and the recognition of emotions in others.

©P

Working with Parents

Getting the children's parents involved was not easy. As one teacher so perceptively put it, and as is so often the case in many schools, "The only parents who come in to see us about their kids are the ones who don't need to." Furthermore, the behaviour-management techniques practised in the school prior to our work had done little to encourage positive parental contact.

Family Night

A couple of months into the program, we organized a casual event for the students' families at the local community centre. This was to be an occasion at which the parents could meet with their children's principal and teachers and hear good things about their children. Signs reading "Come join us for pizza this Friday night at the Community Centre" were posted around the neighbourhood, and the night of the event the place was packed. In many cases, after a lifetime of receiving discouraging notes from the school, it was time for these parents to hear something positive—and *only* something positive—about their child. The positive comments could include anything from increased participation in class discussions, to enthusiasm for a particular subject, to demonstration of leadership qualities, to sports or music ability. I was sure that parents would be receptive to this because a social worker in the community had told me that he had never met any local parents who did not hope for better lives for their children. We discussed with the staff how very important it was for all of us to fuel the parents' hope and pride in their children, as that would, in turn, encourage the parents to say positive things to their children. This would lower their own and the children's anxiety levels, as well as increase the chances for better parent–child social interactions.

As we anticipated, a number of the children became rambunctious at this event. The combination of being together and the noise level, not to mention free pizza, led to a great deal of excitement. The teachers were prepared for this, and redirected the children—for example, by having them help set up or clear away dishes—when the children needed to down-regulate. The teachers also refrained from criticizing parents for being overly harsh with their child. At the outset, we had determined to keep the evening short: we explained at the start that we had the hall for two hours and would end the event on time (which we did). One unexpected and very satisfying result of this get-together was seeing members of the community enjoying each other's company so much that they took steps to plan another family-oriented event independent of the school.

Promoting Social Self-Regulation

- Provide children with collaborative learning experiences to encourage social self-regulation as students help one another working in small groups. In many cases, this will lead students at all levels to show greater concentration on and persistence in their task.

- While classroom demands can be overwhelming, consider why you may be seeing certain behaviours from a student and what can be done to help that student learn to self-regulate.

- Develop children's understanding and vocabulary around social-emotional learning.

- As appropriate, allow children to select their own activities and set their own goals. Autonomy can play an important part in the development of social self-regulation.

- Try to establish a connection with children's parents/caregivers and their community so there is continuity between self-regulation strategies used in and out of the classroom.

- Look for opportunities to promote understanding of others' experiences and feelings.

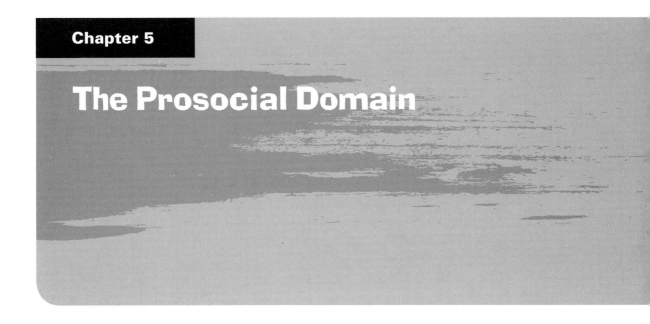

Chapter 5

The Prosocial Domain

Key Attributes of the Prosocial Domain

Children who are optimally regulated in the prosocial domain will demonstrate the following key attributes:

- the ability to help regulate others and to co-regulate with others

- a sense of honesty, both with themselves and with others

- empathy, or the capacity to care about others' feelings and to help them deal with their emotions

- the ability to put the needs and interests of others ahead of their own

- the desire to "do the right thing" and the conviction to act on their convictions

What Is Prosocial Regulation and Why Is It Important?

Jean Twenge

The term *prosocial* refers to those behaviours that are positive, helpful, and intended to promote social acceptance and friendship. For research purposes, the prosocial domain encompasses empathy, altruism, and morality. In this chapter, we will focus primarily on the first of these aspects, in part because since Jean Twenge published her critically acclaimed *Generation Me* (2006), alarm bells have been ringing about children's increasing problems with developing empathy.

©P

Children can be easily overloaded by other children's emotions, or hesitant or even unwilling to respond in a caring manner to another's distress. This lack of skills in the prosocial domain can set off a wave of dysregulating effects across the biological, emotional, cognitive, and social domains of our five-domain model of self-regulation. It is for this reason that helping students to achieve optimal regulation in the prosocial domain is so important. Students with optimal prosocial regulation have a heightened ability to stay calmly focused and alert in the face of stressors at all other levels of our model.

The concern is widespread. In a commencement address in 2006 at Northwestern University in Evanston, Illinois, then Senator Barack Obama told the graduating students:

> Empathy [is] the ability to put ourselves in someone else's shoes, to see the world through the eyes of those who are different from us—the child who's hungry, the laid-off steelworker, the immigrant woman cleaning your dorm room.
>
> As you go on in life, cultivating this quality of empathy will become harder, not easier. There's no community service requirement in the real world; no one forcing you to care....
>
> Not only that—we live in a culture that discourages empathy. A culture that too often tells us our principal goal in life is to be rich, thin, young, famous, safe, and entertained. A culture where those in power too often encourage these selfish impulses.

Obama's statements, with their focus on empathy, raise a number of critical questions for us to keep in mind as we look at co- and self-regulation in the prosocial domain:

- What exactly is empathy?

- Why is empathy so important both for the well-being of children and for those with whom they interact?

- How does a child develop empathy?

- How can we encourage the development of empathy in daily social interactions, both within and outside of our schools?

- What does empathy have to do with self- and co-regulation?

- What does empathy have to do with **bullying**?

- Why is empathy important for learning?

Bullying—physical, verbal, or mental abuse directed at one or more individuals, usually repeatedly, and intended to harm

©P

Let us begin by looking at the first and second of these questions, to which Obama has provided some answers.

The Nature and Importance of Empathy

There is a common perception, reflected in Obama's opening statements above, that empathy is simply "putting ourselves in someone else's shoes" and then feeling to an extent what that person is feeling. These are important points, but they do not reflect the following very critical aspects of empathy:

- *caring* about someone else's emotions (e.g., being genuinely concerned when another person is upset)

- *trying to help* others deal with their emotions (e.g., attempting to calm others who are upset and providing them with heartfelt support)

- *distinguishing* between your own and someone else's emotions (e.g., remaining calm yourself in the face of that person's upset)

Clearly, there are two common elements in each of these key aspects of empathy: the emotions that one feels, and connecting with the emotions of someone else. Not surprisingly, then, a deficit in one of them (not caring, for example) can result in emotional and related psychological and behavioural problems, such as low self-esteem or bullying, an issue that will be addressed in greater detail later in this chapter (pp. 114–116). See "What Is Bullying and How Do You Recognize It?," on the next page.

Empathy

Steps to Respect

What Is Bullying and How Do You Recognize It?

Bullying can be broadly defined as physical, verbal, or mental abuse directed at one or more individuals, usually repeatedly, and intended to harm. *Cyberbullying*, or abuse over the internet, involves the last two of these behaviours. Verbal and mental abuse includes behaviours such as name calling, malicious rumour mongering, and excluding (or threatening to exclude) individuals from a group. The research-based Steps to Respect bullying-prevention program lists the indicators shown in Figure 5.1, below, in its Program Guide (Committee for Children, 2005, p. 16) to help teachers and other adults recognize physical bullying and distinguish it from everyday "play fighting, or 'rough-and-tumble' play."

Figure 5.1: Indicators to Distinguish Play Fighting from Bullying

Play Fighting	Bullying
Positive facial expressions (e.g., smiling)	Negative facial expressions (e.g., angry looks)
Voluntary participation	Involuntary participation
Alternated roles (e.g., being chased, then being the chaser)	Fixed roles (being either the aggressor or the victim)
Tempered force	Aggressive force
Children stay together after playing	Children separate after an encounter

Self-regulatory problems in the prosocial domain generally reveal themselves in a student's difficulties joining in with others in one-on-one and larger-group social interactions. Classrooms and schools are, of course, replete with such situations. These students may be unable to fit in and be active and well-adjusted members of their class because they lack empathy, a key aspect of optimal regulation in the prosocial domain.

Second Step: Social Skills for Early Childhood–Grade 8

Second Step is a comprehensive program designed to help students from preschool through to Grade 8 develop core social-emotional skills, such as problem solving, self-talk, emotion management, active listening, and empathy. The research-based program is delivered via grade-level lessons and activities and is comprehensive in both its range of concepts and product support. In recent years, the Second Step program has expanded its Kindergarten to Grade 5 program to include a focus on self-regulation.

The Second Step program is published by Committee for Children, a non-profit agency, and has been used in 70 countries around the world. The constant message of the program—wherever and whenever it is employed—is that children can be taught the skills they need to keep them safe, lead healthy physical and social lives, and improve their school achievements.

Second Step

The Middle Years Development Instrument

The Middle Years Development Instrument was developed by the Human Early Learning Partnership (affiliated with the University of British Columbia), the United Way of the Lower Mainland (BC), and the Vancouver School Board. It is designed for students 6 to 12 years of age and is administered in Grade 4. It consists of 71 questions related to five areas: social and emotional development, connectedness, school experiences, physical health and well-being, and constructive use of after-school time. Participation is voluntary and all results are anonymous. Reflective of the partners who devised the questionnaire, results are provided to the class, school, and community to ensure that programs reflect the needs of students.

The Middle Years Development Instrument

The Role of Empathy in the Evolution of Humans

Some researchers have speculated that the need for "belongingness" lies at the heart of our species, establishing its capacity to survive (Baumeister & Leary, 1995; King, 2007). Consider the following observations:

> We humans crave emotional connection with others. This deep desire to connect can be explained by the long evolutionary history we shared with other primates, the monkeys and apes.… The most profound, indeed the most stirring transformations in the evolutionary history of Homo sapiens involve what does not fossilize and what is only sometimes made tangible: belongingness. Belongingness is mattering to someone who matters to you.… Relating emotionally to others shapes the very quality of our lives.
>
> Belongingness, then, is a useful shorthand term for the undeniable reality that humans of all ages, in all societies, thrive in relation to others. (King, 2007, pp. 1–2)

Here, biological anthropologist Barbara King describes what is arguably the most important of all qualities for what it means to be human: the capacity that enabled our hominid ancestors to survive and, as she puts it, to "thrive" as individuals and as a society through the emotional connectedness that is at the heart of empathy. This view, supported by the work of other evolutionary theorists such as de Waal (2002, 2009), Dugatkin (2006), and Wilson and Wilson (2007), reveals the limits of what is known in primatology as the "Machiavellian Intelligence Hypothesis" (MIH).

As its name implies, MIH emphasizes the larger role played by less positive aspects of behaviour—manipulation and deception—in contrast to the supposed lesser role of empathy in the growth of the primate brain. Some researchers have also linked bullying behaviour to MIH (Sutton, Smith, & Swettenham, 1999). King and the theorists cited in the previous paragraph argue, however, that the processing demands involved in complex social interactions go far beyond these calculated, aggressive, self-serving ones envisaged by MIH.

©P

The Role of Empathy in Co-Regulation

Social interactions involve much more than just communicating bits of information. They involve the expression of intentions, attitudes, desires, fears, and the like. Successful social interactions occur when one child not only knows, but also connects with and cares about, what another child is feeling. Generally speaking, as described in Chapter 4, the more two children "resonate" positively with each other emotionally, the better they will co-regulate; and the better they co-regulate, the more they will turn to one another for the support that encourages the development of empathy. Notably, some researchers have characterized empathy as a "core temperamental trait," but, alarmingly, one that is increasingly under threat.

Empathy as a Core Temperamental Trait

Many psychologists think of empathy as a core temperamental trait because it plays a central role in a child's prosocial development (Berkowitz, 1998; Eisenberg et al., 1991; Kagan, 1984). Viewing empathy in this way draws attention to its robust stability if established from a young age. In other words, a child who is highly empathetic at the time he starts school is very likely to be a highly empathetic teenager who is very likely to be an empathetic adult.

The Prosocial Child

On the other hand, a child who is uncaring or aggressive in Grade 1 is very likely to demonstrate the same (or worse) dysregulated behaviour in Grade 6 if her "empathy deficiency" is not addressed. Rather than attributing this deficiency to the child's genes, we should instead consider possible contributing factors in her classroom and home environments, such as

- excessive discipline at school or at home, which does *not* foster the development of empathy (O'Keefe, 2005)

- overindulgent parenting, which avoids regulating children's behaviour and encourages self-centredness, the antithesis of empathy (Galton & MacBeath, 2008)

- the celebration of narcissism and self-aggrandizement on television and in other media, which also promotes self-centredness (Twenge, 2006; Twenge & Campbell, 2009)

- an overly competitive school and/or after-school environment that prizes individual accomplishments at the expense of group sports and achievements that exist outside of competitions

If such conditions remain unchanged, the child will likely continue to exhibit the same, if not worse, behaviour right through school and into adulthood. The earlier we change such conditions for the better, helping her to develop the core temperamental trait of empathy, the better the chance of that child blossoming.

Let us eavesdrop for a moment on the following exchange between two students from opposing teams after the final game of a tournament that went into overtime:

> **Student A:** Fantastic game for you. Congrats! But what a bummer for us to lose in overtime.
>
> **Student B:** Didn't we play great? We sure beat you guys.

Student A is clearly generous in her congratulations, sharing some of her peer's happiness while expressing her own upset at losing. Student B, on the other hand, is focused solely on his happiness at winning, oblivious to Student A's upset. Needless to say, there is not likely to be any sustained positive interaction between these two students. Had Student B responded as follows, however, such an interaction would likely have developed: "Yeah, I think it was a great game for both teams. We both played hard. Good luck in your next game."

Discordances in empathy can be especially pronounced when two children are at different levels of emotional development. This point applies not just to the intensity of the emotions that the two children feel, but also to the very emotions that each experiences. For example, a child who has never experienced envy is likely to find it difficult to interact with someone who is demonstrating this emotion, because there is little common ground for making a connection. Very simply, the more a child has experienced the emotions that another is experiencing, the more the child can empathize with those emotions (Eysenck & Eysenck, 1985).

Furthermore, empathy is based on one's own experiences of what it feels like to be in a certain situation, as well as the ability to empathize with some emotions more than with others. Student C, for example, may be able to imagine herself in Student D's shoes in an upsetting situation, but may not feel what the latter is feeling because she simply would not feel that way in the same circumstances. As a result, Student C is not really connecting with Student D, and might actually dysregulate the latter further by perhaps telling him not to be so foolish by becoming upset.

No doubt, most of us will have had the experience of playing the part of dysregulator with our children. As adults, it is all too easy to dismiss a child's fears (for example, a child's fear of the dark or of trying something new) because we know there is no basis for the fear or we want to minimize the child's anxiety, or perhaps both elements are at play. In the end, our lack of empathy does nothing to ease the child's anxiety. Rather, it increases it—his fears are real to him and now he feels a sense of shame or embarrassment because of our response.

So how do we change this in the classroom (and for many of us as parents)? Perhaps it is easiest to go back to Obama's statement and the oft-heard line of putting ourselves in someone else's shoes—in this case, the child's. In the example above, if we put ourselves in the child's shoes (and perhaps even remember back to our own fear of the dark!), we may see that there are other ways to handle the child's anxiety. Are there strategies he can use to help him cope (for example, leave the door open or keep a flashlight handy)? In this instance, we decrease the child's anxiety at the same time that we help him develop self-regulatory behaviours by providing him with strategies that will allow him to master his anxiety.

Helping Children Develop the Ability to See Other Perspectives

The Demands of the Prosocial Domain

As with all of the other domains, the prosocial domain can be very stressful. In fact, this domain can be characterized as *intrinsically* stressful. It invariably involves, to a greater or lesser degree and depending on the individual, conflicts between what one child is feeling or wants and what another child is feeling or wants. When you think about it, we start making many different kinds of prosocial demands on children from the moment they enter an early childhood setting and, even earlier, with their siblings at home. We want them to play nicely together, share willingly, think about others, and wait their turn. As they grow older, we pressure them to get involved in extracurricular school activities, such as participating in sports and volunteering for charity drives.

What makes these prosocial demands stressful for children is the internal struggle that they often experience: the effort they must make to resist a selfish impulse, to put the interests of others ahead of their own. Children need a great deal of support in this regard, some more so than others. Otherwise, they can easily become dysregulated in all five of the domains, often most publicly and disruptively in the prosocial domain. In other words, the prosocial domain is where the effects of impulsivity, unmodulated negative emotions, inattentiveness, and deficient social intelligence are especially manifest (Blackburn, 1993; Gottfredson & Hirschi, 1990; Hirschi, 2004). This is also the domain where, as a teacher, you are in a position to provide the regulating guidance needed to allow your students' self- and co-regulating behaviours to flourish. Rose is such a teacher, and we will now turn our attention to what occurred in her classroom.

Applications in the Classroom

Scenario

Rose had mixed feelings about her new job as a Grade 4 teacher in a socially complex school environment. On the positive side, her principal was supportive, and the school was appealing, with large, bright classrooms; an up-to-date library resource centre; and an inviting, well-equipped playground. Rose also liked her group of 23 students, who came from a variety of cultural backgrounds. However, her students did not demonstrate much empathy toward each other—working with one another on projects only because they were required to and tending to bond only with close friends. Rose also noticed a fair amount of bullying behaviour among them, some of it involving ethnic slurs.

©P

As was the case with the original conditions at the school we looked at in the last chapter, Rose's school emphasized a behaviour-management approach to dealing with any misbehaviour. Its zero-tolerance policy regarding ethnic slurs, for example, was strictly enforced. Rose understood the necessity of this policy, of course. However, she found the overall approach to this and other discipline-related issues decidedly deficient in recognizing the crucial importance of empathy—and prosocial behaviour generally—for encouraging positive, sustained interactions inside and outside of school.

What surprised Rose was that the school was supposedly committed to the prosocial goals of character education (see "Character Development Programs, or Character and Citizenship Education," next page). However, this involved little more than colourful posters displayed around the school with slogans such as the following:

- Character makes a difference.

- Respect is one of the highest qualities we can have—for others and for ourselves.

- We are all part of the same community and must do our share to help each other.

Rose fully agreed with all that these posters were promoting, but the students barely glanced at the slogans. This was not surprising since there was no coherent, viable program as such at the school for supporting and achieving these prosocial goals. (A common workplace parallel—the ever-present, oft-ignored Mission Statement!)

As it was, Rose had read *Generation Me* (mentioned earlier on p. 93), and she agreed with Twenge's argument that the narcissism promoted by television and other media seriously undermines prosocial behaviours. It did not take Rose long, through chats with her students, to determine that they did indeed watch *lots* of television. In her mind, there was little doubt that this was a contributing factor to the general lack of empathy she noticed, manifested in bullying and other behaviours. Other important factors, stemming from her own observations and from conversations with her students, fellow teachers, and parents, were the influence of peer pressure to "fit in"; differences in values among her culturally diverse students; and problematic situations at home. Rose was determined that something had to be done to encourage more empathy among her students.

She had heard of our centre's school programs through a colleague at another school. With her principal's approval, she approached us and we outlined a program for her to promote prosocial behaviour in her classroom.

Character Education

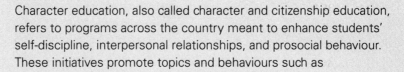

Character Development Programs, or Character and Citizenship Education

Character education, also called character and citizenship education, refers to programs across the country meant to enhance students' self-discipline, interpersonal relationships, and prosocial behaviour. These initiatives promote topics and behaviours such as

- equity and respect for diversity

- school culture, civility, and safety

- volunteer activities

- civic involvement

- engagement in social-justice issues

Examples of these programs include Alberta Education's "Heart of the Matter: Character and Citizenship Education" initiative; the Safe Schools Manitoba partnership, supported by Manitoba's Ministry of Education and other Manitoba government and civic agencies; and the Ontario Ministry of Education's *Finding Common Ground: Character Development in Ontario Schools, K–12* (2008).

Encouraging Self-Regulation: A Classroom Makeover and Yoga
The prosocial program we recommended for Rose kicked off, in fact, with activities to encourage self-regulation in the biological and emotional domains. This reflects the key principle of this resource: to work on any one domain of our five-domain model of self-regulation, we have to work on all of the domains. In this case, the activities were meant to instill the calm and focus Rose's students needed to improve their behaviour in the prosocial domain.

We first shared with Rose the details on Doris's classroom makeover covered in Chapter 1 (pp. 11–18). Much of it did not interest Rose because of the grade level challenges, but she did pick up several ideas. Rose asked her students to help her remove their least favourite posters and pictures from the classroom walls. As it turned out, the students liked very few of them, so this resulted in walls devoid of many of the more distracting and, for some, overly stimulating images. She also picked up on the idea of using tennis balls on the bottom of desk and chair legs. Over time, Rose noticed fewer instances of biologically dysregulated behaviour (hyper- and hypoarousal), as the students generally became calmer.

We also shared with Rose the classroom scenario we covered in Chapter 2 on self-regulation in the emotional domain (pp. 31–43). As a result, Rose introduced a weekly yoga session in a cleared space in the middle of the classroom, and, once again, she called on her students to help her. She was able to borrow mats from the gym, and noticed something interesting: the act of helping her get the mats and move the tables and chairs helped prepare the students for their yoga sessions. They began calming down as they performed these tasks. To Rose's surprise, a number of students asked for more sessions and instruction in new poses. She was also surprised at how much her students *enjoyed* calming down through yoga and how much they looked forward to it. This salutary effect of *the anticipation of calm* has, in fact, been corroborated by researchers (Fogel, 2009).

Tackling Empathy Deficit: Movies

To begin directly tackling their empathy deficit, we suggested to Rose that she show her students some carefully chosen movies, alerting them before viewing to certain themes, especially as they related to empathy. She was then to pick up on those themes in a class discussion after each film, encouraging the students to talk about how the action reflected the themes. Generally speaking and understandably, children tend to focus on action and entertainment value more than they do on a film's more subtle "empathy content."

After each movie, Rose would encourage discussion based on answers to questions such as the following:

- What do you think [character's name] felt at that moment in the movie when she [or he] was interacting with [another character's name]?

- Why do you think she [or he] felt that way?

- Would you have felt that way in a similar situation? Why or why not?

- Have you ever felt differently than others did in a particular situation (for example, happy when others were feeling unhappy)? Why was that? Do you think your feelings were appropriate for the situation? If not, what do you think you could do to respond more appropriately the next time to the same or a similar situation?

Tackling Empathy Deficit Template

The first movie Rose showed was *Beauty and the Beast* (Trousdale et al., 1991). She chose this movie because many students were preoccupied with how they looked, and would tease each other for anything considered odd in someone's appearance. Before the viewing, Rose explained that the film was the story of a prince who gets turned into a hideous beast by an enchantress because of his treatment of a beggar (who is, in fact, the enchantress in disguise). A beautiful young woman called Belle eventually sees past his looks, however, realizing how unhappy he is. She also recognizes that he has good qualities, and her own goodness helps those qualities to blossom and thereby transform him.

After the film, Rose encouraged her students to explore empathy-related questions, using evidence from the movie to support their thinking:

- Why does the enchantress turn the prince into a beast? [Because he is self-centred and behaves in a cold and heartless way toward her in her disguise as a beggar.]

- How does the prince feel when he is turned into a beast? [He becomes very unhappy because his self-centredness makes him very concerned about his appearance as a beast.]

- What is Belle's first reaction when she first encounters the prince as a beast? [She sees him as nothing more than a beast, hideous both on the outside and the inside.]

- What is Belle's later reaction to the beast? [She comes to understand that he is unhappy and that, in fact, he is capable of being

©P

kind and generous. Because of her empathetic understanding of him, she is kind to him.]

- How does the beast respond to Belle's kindness and selflessness? [He wants to be more like her. As a result, his latent kindness and generosity manifest themselves when he empathizes with her over her anguish for her father, who has been unjustly imprisoned.]

- How does Belle respond to the beast's concern for her? [She comes to love him.]

- What happens as a result? [The beast is transformed back to being human, now a more empathetic one, and worthy of Belle.]

- Have you ever made an initial judgment about someone, based only on how that person looked or talked, but then changed your opinion when you got to know the individual better? What was it about that person that made you change your mind?

Notice how very careful Rose was about nudging the students to tease out the theme of empathy embedded in the film and then relate it to their own lives.

As a follow-up to the film, Rose formed random groups of four students to discuss this last question:

- What kinds of things do you do to help bring out the best in someone else? [For example, complimenting them on an act of generosity, or helping them to get over their anxiety about performing in a school concert or competing in a basketball or hockey game.]

Rose asked each group to list examples of acts of kindness they had performed or received. For each act, she asked them to identify the incident that sparked the act, and how they felt as generators (or recipients) of the action. Once all of the groups had had a chance to make their list, Rose asked them to come together as a class. She then asked her students to think particularly about the indicators people give, intentionally or otherwise, when they need help or support. The point was to have the students recognize these acts of empathy and help them to increase their ability to recognize the emotions of others and their ability to ease someone's discomfort.

Another movie that Rose showed was *Nanny McPhee* (Jones et al., 2005). She figured, quite correctly, that her students would find the film highly entertaining, and that it would offer an excellent opportunity for them to think and talk about what empathy means.

Rose gave a very brief overview of the movie before she showed it. A widowed father and his seven children are financially supported by his late wife's fearsome and meddling aunt. The father is depressed and incapable of caring for his misbehaving children, who have driven away 17 nannies! His latest hire is Nanny McPhee and, in the course of the movie, she gets the children to behave themselves, and eventually she herself is transformed.

After showing the film, Rose asked her students the following questions:

- Why were the children behaving so badly in the earlier part of the movie? Did they just need to be disciplined to behave properly? [Their mother's death had deeply upset them. Disciplining them would not get them to behave properly. They needed the adults around them to understand how upset they were.]

- How much good or harm was their great-aunt, Lady Adelaide Stitch, doing to the family? [She thought that she was helping them by being firm, but the family actually seemed to be falling apart because of the stresses she was imposing.]

- How is Nanny McPhee different from Lady Adelaide? [They are opposites. Instead of punishing the children or threatening them with punishment, Nanny alerts them to the consequences of their actions, encouraging them to take responsibility for what they do.]

- Deep down, what exactly did the children need from Nanny McPhee? [Someone who truly empathized with the pain they were feeling at the loss of their mother—and someone who could help them come to terms with their grief and become more prosocial in their behaviour.]

- What is the meaning of Nanny McPhee's change of appearance near the end of the movie? [Her frightening, witch-like appearance in the early part of the film reflected how the children initially saw her, because they did not recognize that she was, in

©P

fact, deeply empathetic with their feelings and what they needed. As the film progresses and the children come to recognize this fact, Nanny McPhee's physical appearance gradually changes, and by the end of the film, she has turned into a beautiful young woman.]

- Have you ever been so upset or sad about a situation that you did not want or know how to talk about it? Why was that? Looking back now on the situation, what do you feel you might have done to encourage yourself to talk clearly about it?

Rose asked her students to think about how Nanny McPhee helped the children to take responsibility for their actions. She then posed the following question:

- Has anyone ever helped you to understand how important it is to take responsibility for the consequences of your actions? In what ways did you find this helpful?

Rose then drew her students' attention to the character education posters around the school and asked them whether it was easier for them to understand the posters now. If they could make a poster on this part of character education—taking responsibility—what would it look like? Students were given the option of working on their own or with a partner to design a personal character education poster, working on it in several language arts and arts periods.

Perhaps the most successful of all these movies for Rose's main purpose—getting her students to appreciate the importance of empathy—was *Ice Age* (Saldanha et al., 2002). The film, as Rose introduced it, is about three prehistoric animals who are very different from one another but eventually become friends: an annoying sloth (Sid), who intrudes on others and rushes thoughtlessly into danger; a quiet, withdrawn woolly mammoth (Manny), who is actually strong and brave; and a sabre-toothed tiger (Diego), who is always saying hurtful things. The only thing these three animals have in common is that, for one reason or another, they are all outsiders who have been driven to band together by their need for mutual support. For the three animals to become true friends, however, they have to learn not just how to tolerate, but also how to trust and rely on one another. What the film so vividly depicts is how, in the words of one of the characters, they "become their own herd" through the connection of empathy. In other words, they come to understand and support each other's emotional needs.

Ice Age stimulated a lively discussion about the importance of friends and what it takes to form true friendships. Most of the students noted that each of the main characters performs a heroic act to save one of his friends. One of the students' favourite scenes was when Sid tricks Diego into jumping into the river by convincing him that he really could swim. This was something with which Rose's students could identify: how they could help their friends do something they were really afraid of trying by convincing them that they could do it.

Importantly, *Ice Age* also helped Rose initiate a discussion with her students about developing self- and co-regulation in the prosocial domain. In other words, she did not want to coerce her students into behaving in an empathetic manner, but rather to get them to *want* to be empathetic and to become more aware of the voluntary regulatory processes involved. As part of this discussion, too, Rose alerted her students to the "belongingness drive" noted earlier (p. 98)—King's characterization of empathy as the quality that binds humans to each other, and that has enabled us to survive and thrive as a species since our earliest days.

Movies That Promote Prosocial Behaviour

Understanding Empathy in Animals

After the preceding discussions, we suggested that Rose ask her students whether they thought animals could feel empathy. Given the amount of time that children spend watching television shows that blur the line between animals and humans, it was not surprising that Rose's students were all were convinced that animals were just like us when it comes to empathy. (This view is commonly known as *anthropomorphism*.)

We then recommended that Rose tell her students that some scientists (Budiansky, 2003; Wynne, 2004) believe that animals do not feel any empathy, because they have few if any emotions—being little more than "reflex machines" that simply react to stimuli.

©P

Animal Behaviour and Emotions

To counter this view, Rose told her students in simple terms about the criticism of the Machiavellian Intelligence Hypothesis (MIH) that was covered earlier in this chapter (p. 98). She told her students about the work of the primatologist Frans de Waal (2002 with Stephanie D. Preston; 2009), who began his career studying apes from the MIH perspective but eventually came to recognize examples of empathetic behaviour among them: for example, sharing tasty treats with each other and even hugging and kissing to make up after fights. De Waal became convinced that these animals were demonstrating true empathy, not just basic reflexive behaviour. In his view, apes really do resonate with each other emotionally and express caring.

Rose then showed her class a video of evolutionary biologist Marc Bekoff talking about emotions in animals (Bekoff, 1999). In this video, Bekoff explains how animals with a similar brain structure and physiology to humans (for example, dogs, cats, elephants, wolves, and dolphins) experience emotions similar to ours, even though their feelings may be less complex. In the video, he states that he came to this conclusion by closely observing both domesticated and wild animals, often videotaping their behaviour to look at it closely and repeatedly. At one point in the video, he shows a clip of two dogs who seem to be fighting. At first, it looks like they might have to be separated before they hurt each other. Bekoff points out, however, that this "fight" is really carefully structured: for example, the dogs use a "play bow" to get permission to engage in the play fight, and each dog knows how hard to bite without hurting and when to back off. Once we understand the significance of these behaviours, Bekoff points out, we begin to understand the happiness the dogs are experiencing as they play fight, and how an interaction like this builds their trust in each other and what Bekoff refers to as a "wild justice."

After the class viewed the video, Rose gave her students a homework assignment to read Bekoff's *Psychology Today* blog entitled "Animal Emotions" (2011) and Barbara King's NPR blog entitled "Humans and Other Animals" (2011) to find examples of empathy in animals. Their assignment was to tell a story about animal empathy that they found in one of the blogs to help them convince someone who believes that animals have no emotions that he or she is wrong. Rose also encouraged her students to include examples from their own experiences with animals, for example, with pets or during a visit to a zoo. The students loved this assignment. One student told a story about how his dog hurt his paw and the family's pet cat licked it. Another student followed this up by saying, "I was sick in bed one time and my dog came and licked my face, and then he went and lay down at the foot of the bed and stayed with me like that for hours."

Understanding and Encouraging Empathy

Using the Roots of Empathy Program
The next set of questions that Rose wanted her students to think and talk about concerned the early development of empathy in children:

- How do children become empathetic?

- How early does this start?

- How can we help ourselves and others become more empathetic?

To help Rose and her students address these questions, we contacted Roots of Empathy and had them introduce their program into her class.

SPOTLIGHT

The Roots of Empathy Program

Roots of Empathy

In the Roots of Empathy program, developed for K–8 classes, a parent from a school's neighbourhood brings an infant, ranging in age from two to four months, into a class in September, and returns to the class every three weeks, always with the baby, for a total 27 visits over the course of the year. The basic premise of the program is that as the children watch a parent's loving care of a baby, they observe and comment on the growth of empathy in both the child and in the parent–child relationship.

An instructor trained in child development guides the children's observations and conversations during the visit. Over the course of the year, the children learn about such things as temperament, attachment, infant development, and the meaning of affect signals.

©P

Rose's Grade 4 students became entranced during these family visits. At one session, the children sat absolutely spellbound as a four-month-old baby boy tried to sit up: he propped himself up on his arms, stayed upright for around 15 seconds, then suddenly collapsed and began crying. Amid their gasps, some students asked questions, eliciting answers and comments from other students and the Roots of Empathy instructor. Some examples:

Student: Why did he fall over?
Student: He's not big enough.
Student: I think he's not strong enough to stay up.
Instructor: Correct. His muscles need to develop more before he can sit upright like you're doing. Your trunk muscles are now strong enough for you to do so.

Student: Why is he crying?
Student: I think he may have hurt himself.
Student: No. He's just mad because he can't sit up yet.
Instructor: That's it. He's feeling frustrated because he can't stay upright.

Student: Why does he want to sit up so badly?
Student: I really don't think he's trying hard enough.
Student: Maybe so he can see us better.
Instructor: That's just about right. He wants to be higher so that he can see all of you guys and everything that's going on in this room.

Student: Can we do anything to help him sit up?
Student: My cousin is almost a year old and she still can't sit up. She must be really frustrated!
Student: What about putting him in one of those bouncing baby seats? I've seen them on television. It would sit him almost straight up.
Instructor: Great idea! Doing that would help him see all of you and what's going on around him better. That should make him happier.

Over the next few visits, the students observed how the parent soothed her baby whenever he got frustrated, and how she supported him physically until the time came when he was finally able to sit up and stay up on his own. The class responded to this feat by cheering! The baby himself responded to the cheers with a huge smile, which seemed to transport everyone in the room into a state of shared bliss—what the "belongingness drive" is all about.

What really deepened the students' understanding of empathy was the amount of time the instructor spent talking with them about what empathy is and why it is so important to helping human beings get along with each other. By the end of the Roots of Empathy program, the students really understood how empathy grows further from experiencing empathy, and from learning how to "read," from their behaviour, what other people are thinking and feeling.

Reading Fiction
Throughout the year, Rose used Gwen Dewar's "Teaching Empathy: Evidence-Based Tips for Fostering Empathy in Children" (2009). We encouraged her to explore the following questions with her students, which are suggested by the tips in Dewar's article.

Teaching Empathy

- What does someone look like when he or she is angry? sad? happy? frightened? bored? interested? What is it exactly in that person's look that makes you think so?

- How do you think those feelings influence that person's behaviour?

- How might a person recover from something really upsetting? In what ways might you help that person to recover?

- How hard is it to show care for someone when you are having a terrible day?

- What does it feel like to be bullied?

- What do you feel like when you see someone being bullied?

Helping Children Understand Bullying

Since some of the issues raised by these questions (bullying, in particular) can be difficult for children to handle in the classroom, we advised Rose to find creative and non-threatening ways to explore them. She immediately thought of having her students read and respond to fictional stories. These offer opportunities to focus on empathy (or lack of empathy) in characters and situations at a safe remove from students' own lives, while encouraging them to address topics they find troubling. In keeping with this approach, Rose stressed to her students that all references had to be to the fictional stories they were reading. No examples of specific children or stressful situations in their class or school were to be mentioned. The last thing she wanted to do was deal with prosocial themes at the cost of dysregulating any of the students.

Self- and Co-Regulation and Bullying

Discipline on its own is not enough to deal with a bullying problem. Everyone concerned—the teacher, perpetrator, victim, and witnesses—needs to be sensitized to the emotions triggered in the situation, and to learn how to deal with them through self- and coregulation. Most important is the need to work on the underlying factors—the hyperarousal, emotional dysregulation, and underdeveloped prosocial skills—that have led up to the act of bullying.

A book that Rose found especially helpful for addressing bullying, for example, was Trudy Ludwig's *Confessions of a Former Bully* (2010). She particularly liked its unique point of view. Through the voice of Katie, who is sent to the school counsellor for her bullying, Ludwig is able to deal with some of the more subtle aspects of bullying. Katie confesses at one point that she always thought that bullying only referred to physical acts. She had never realized (as noted earlier, on p. 96) that saying mean things, spreading nasty rumours, and excluding someone from a group—including doing so online—can be sometimes as harmful as, or even more harmful than, physical bullying. This was the perfect message to get the students to think about the effects of their actions on someone else's feelings.

Reading *Confessions of a Former Bully* resulted in a valuable learning opportunity for the students. One of them observed, "It's really good the way Katie starts to think about why she was bullying her friends." Soon everyone in the room was talking about why Katie was being a bully, that is, because she felt bad about herself and thought that she would feel better if she made someone else feel bad. In the staff room at lunchtime afterwards, Rose told one of her colleagues about a student who was a bit prone to bullying smaller kids suddenly remarking, "It's almost like Katie feels bad about bullying her friends, but the worse she feels about this, the more she does it!" For Rose, probably the best part of the class discussion was when a student piped up: "Katie really needed to learn that it was just as bad to say mean things

Dealing with Bullying

PREVNet is a national network of Canadian researchers, nongovernmental organizations, and government agencies that work together to stop bullying.

about other kids on Facebook as it is to say mean things to their face on the playground." As Rose later told another colleague, "You could hear a pin drop when the kid said this. You could just about hear the wheels turning in their brains as they all digested this comment."

Empathy-Focused Children's Books

Rose also had her students read *The Mouse and the Motorcycle* by Beverly Cleary (1990), the acclaimed author of children's books. The story is about Ralph, an adventurous mouse who lives in a rundown hotel. One day, a family comes to stay at the hotel and, to Ralph's amazement, Keith, their little boy, is able to understand and talk to Ralph. The two strike up an unlikely friendship, which culminates in Keith letting Ralph ride his toy motorcycle, but only at night when he cannot be seen by others. Ralph agrees to this condition. One day, through a series of calamitous daytime events, Ralph ends up losing the motorcycle as he tries to escape from the housekeeper's vacuum.

When Keith learns of this, he loses all trust in Ralph and their friendship becomes strained, almost beyond repair. Then one night Keith becomes very ill, and his parents are unable to find an Aspirin to bring his fever down. Ralph embarks on a heroic adventure to find an Aspirin somewhere in the hotel. He finally succeeds at great personal risk, and when Keith feels better as a result, he learns what Ralph did for him. In gratitude, he gives the now-found motorcycle to Ralph as a present.

Using Stories to Help Children Develop Empathy

Rose's students loved the story. Just about everyone had had an experience with a friend that involved trust and gratitude, so they could really relate to how Ralph and Keith felt. There was a particularly fruitful exchange between some students who thought that what Ralph did was unforgiveable and others who thought that Keith was not being fair to Ralph because he never even asked why the mouse had needed to use the motorcycle to save his own life. Some seemed to feel that if someone let you down, you could never trust them again. Others felt that the mark of a real friend was to forgive someone, even if they had let you down. Everyone agreed that trust was essential for friendship.

Two comments in particular reflected for Rose these students' understanding of empathy:

> **Student A:** Keith had more empathy than most boys his age. That's why he could understand Ralph, and that's why he forgave him and gave him the motorcycle in the end.

©P

Student B: I don't think Ralph really had that much empathy for Keith at the start. All he really wanted to do was show Keith that he could still be trusted. But then he started to think about Keith and not about himself, and in the end the only thing that mattered to him was helping Keith get better. That's why they became friends again.

Responding to Positive Role Models

In addition to using fiction in her program, Rose had her students focus on empathy in "real-life" situations through looking at and being inspired by the prosocial behaviour of positive role models. Her main example of a positive role model was Craig Kielburger. She used a video to help her tell the students his story. She emphasized that he was not much older than them (12 at the time) when he read a newspaper story about a Pakistani boy who had been forced into child labour at the age of four and later, at the age of 12, murdered. Kielburger took the article to his school, showed it to some of his friends, and together they formed the group "Twelve-Twelve-Year-Olds" to fight against child labour. Eventually, this group grew into the international organization Free the Children. When he was 13 years old, Kielburger held a press conference at which he argued that Canada had a moral responsibility to campaign against child labour. Jean Chrétien, the Canadian prime minister at the time, agreed to support this campaign. As a result of Kielburger's efforts, Canada has now become a major force in combatting child labour.

Positive Role Models

Rose's students became very excited about the idea of doing something similar to what Craig Kielburger had done at a young age. One of them found an online story about the advocacy network Mobilising for Malaria and its campaign to bring treated anti-malarial tents into African villages. Inspired by this, some students suggested that they form their own group, modelled on Kielburger's, the "Ten Ten-Year Olds," and go to Kenya. Rose was bowled over by their enthusiasm, but she realized that she needed to steer them into prosocial action that would be more realistic, closer to home, and include everyone in the class. The local library offered such an opportunity with its "Reading Buddies" program, and it had been advertising for volunteers to help kids in Grade 2 who were having trouble with their reading. This turned out to be the perfect way to help Rose's students improve their reading skills while getting them involved in a community effort and enhancing their self-esteem.

Advocacy Networks
Reading Buddies Programs

Giving Children Opportunities to Help Others

Guiding Children to Self- and Co-Regulate

- Look for opportunities to extend children's understanding of empathy. For example, if someone makes a sarcastic comment in class, discuss the effects of sarcasm experienced by the person who is the target of the comment and others who hear the comment. Typically, the effects of such behaviour affect the larger group in a negative way. Explore the motivations for the behaviour and discuss alternatives.

- Literature provides a way to introduce children to the concept of empathy at the primary grades and to extend students' understanding of the concept at the junior and intermediate grades and beyond. For example, providing primary students with the opportunity to read about children in other countries helps them to make the first important realization that children in other countries, although they may eat different foods, dress differently, and follow different customs, are like them and that the similarities they share outweigh the differences. For older students, literature offers the chance to experience empathy though characters and stories. At any grade, discussions of literature are key to increasing student understanding of empathy.

- Help children to explore the *motivations* and effects of bullying behaviour, so that the exploration extends beyond the typical examination of the effects of bullying on the victim to the reasons why people bully. This provides students with the opportunity to see that the roots of bullying are not in the bully's strengths but in his or her need to increase feelings of self-esteem, power, and so on.

- Increase awareness of bullying—and your "no tolerance" policy—with parents and others in the community. Hold meetings on the topic, as needed.

- Have the class work together on an anti-bullying "contract," which all students then sign to indicate their commitment to it.

©P

- The chapter looked at one young social entrepreneur who has made a difference, Craig Kielburger. There are a number of student groups that have also made remarkable contributions through activism. Students can be encouraged to research these initiatives.

- Support of initiatives needs to be adopted by school staff and have district support. Help your students to define an initiative that is age- and resource-appropriate for them. Provide the support they will need to get official approval from your school and district administration so that they can follow through on their activism.

- At the junior and intermediate grades, promote student awareness of community initiatives that rely on volunteers, such as local food banks and animal shelters. While some students will be too young or not be in a position to volunteer, exposure to the number of organizations and their reliance on volunteers promotes an understanding that the health of a society relies on the contributions its members make to help those less advantaged.

Social Entrepreneurs

Chapter 6

Self-Regulation and Special Education

Special education is one of the most challenging areas for educators. The wide range of issues that need to be addressed in this area can be overwhelming, not to mention the accompanying requirements of customized education programs for students with special needs (see "Special Education Programs in Canada," below). At the same time, it is important to recognize that students in special education programs share the same rights and desires as other children. And, as with all students, the better we can tailor our classroom practices to match each child's existing strengths while providing additional support as necessary, the better we can assist each one to fulfill his or her potential.

S P O T L I G H T

Special Education Programs in Canada

Education Programs for Students with Special Needs

Virtually all school authorities in Canada are required to develop customized education programs for students with special needs (McBride, 2008). These programs have various names, including Individualized Program Plan (IPP) in Alberta; Personal Program Plan (PPP) in Saskatchewan; and Individual Education Plan (IEP), the designation used in British Columbia, Manitoba, Newfoundland, and Ontario. While program specifics vary from province to province, they

■ ■ ■

all recognize that accommodations must be made for students identified with physical, intellectual, communicational, or multiple exceptionalities, such as autism. After identification of the exceptionality (or exceptionalities), each of these programs calls for the close tracking, through regular reporting, of the progress of the student. Classroom teachers are usually responsible for this reporting and for identifying the need for additional assistance from (and team cooperation among) other professionals, such as psychologists, speech-language pathologists, and occupational therapists. All programs encourage the close involvement of parents in addressing the special education needs of their children.

Self-regulation helps students with special needs to fulfill their potential, as it does all students. It is worth recalling the following six critical capacities required for optimal self-regulation noted earlier in the Introduction to this resource (p. xiii):

- when feeling calmly focused and alert, the ability to know that one is calm and alert

- when one is stressed, the ability to recognize what is causing that stress

- the ability to recognize stressors both within and outside the classroom

- the desire to deal with those stressors

- the ability to develop strategies for dealing with those stressors

- the ability to recover efficiently and effectively from dealing with stressors

While the above capacities apply to all children, we need to be especially mindful of their importance for those with special education needs. In doing so, we recognize the critical role that self-regulation can play in helping to address those needs. This is not to suggest that the *cause* of these children's challenges is a problem of self-regulation; rather, that problems in self-regulation are a *downstream* consequence of the complex and highly variable causes of developmental, psychological, and behavioural problems. The key point here is that difficulties in self-regulation can significantly exacerbate the problems of a child with special education needs; conversely, the ability to self-regulate can help to lessen the consequences of such problems.

Children with special needs often require more scaffolding than other children to develop the critical capacities identified above. However, the methods of scaffolding are not necessarily very different from those used to support children who are developing typically. In other words, the basic principles of scaffolding theory apply just as much to the child with special needs as they do to any other child, but the scaffolding may need to be more carefully crafted and adjusted to address the additional challenges involved.

The most important lesson to be learned from working with children who have special education needs may be that, as long as we get a child's learning curve to slope upward, however slowly, we need to assume that the upward trajectory will continue. This suggests that educators should always try to create opportunities for all children to develop core emotional, cognitive, social, and prosocial capacities, regardless of the challenges with which they may be coping. To do so is to recognize every child's overall potential and its connection to the remarkable "plasticity" of the brain.

Norman Doidge: The Brain That Changes Itself

The "Plasticity" of the Brain

"Heightened brain plasticity" is a term generally used to refer to the following:

1. Three periods of intense growth and reorganization of the brain: one in the early years, another just before puberty, and one around the age of 18. During these periods of heightened "plasticity," many new neural connections are forged and pruned (Huttenlocher, 2002; Ramachandran, 2011).

2. Functional specializations: for example, violin players have an enlarged area in their motor cortex for the control of their fingers, blind people an enlarged one related to hearing, and experienced cab drivers an enlarged one involved in spatial processing (Doidge, 2007).

©P

3. The brain's remarkable ability to draw on healthy areas to compensate for parts of the brain that might be injured or deficient in some way. Research indicates, for example, that significant brain improvements can occur in young children with autism as a result of intervention (Stieben, Shanker, & Cassenhiser, 2012 in prep). This holds out the hope that similar results can be obtained in areas of learning disorders such as dyslexia that are also thought to be rooted in neural problems.

Social Learning and Children with Special Needs

Of the five domains, it is especially important to help children with special education needs in the social realm. This means more than just helping them to master social skills, however. What we really need to encourage in these children is their *desire* and *ability* to engage in social interactions, which many are predisposed to find very stressful.

Such an approach is supported by research that concludes that *all* children function optimally in the social world if they are driven by interest, curiosity, and delight in doing so, and, as a result, seek out interactions and focus for longer periods (Bruner, 1977; Ninio & Bruner, 2008; Scaife & Bruner, 1975). Drawing from this premise, recent education initiatives such as play-based learning and an inquiry approach to learning offer as much benefit to students with special needs as they do to typically developing children. In other words, all children function optimally when they find social interactions intrinsically rewarding (Bruner, 1985; Pink, 2009). On the other hand, extrinsic rewards (such as the promise of a cookie for completing a task) do little if anything to promote sustained social learning (Deci, Koestner, & Ryan, 1999; Krugalanski, 1978; Lepper, Sagotsky, Dafoe, & Greene, 1982; Lepper, Sethi, Dialdin, & Drake, 1997).

Moreover, as Bruner and others have argued, it is through social interaction that children master the *nuances* of social interaction, such as facial expressions, vocalizations, and gestures. And the better a child grasps the meaning of such communicative behaviours, the less stress she will experience in social interactions, and the more she will use similar nonverbal and verbal tools to initiate and co-regulate social interactions (Bruner, 1983; Greenspan & Shanker, 2004). A critical reason why children with special needs find social encounters particularly stressful is because they have not fully mastered the use of these nuanced tools, and hence shy away from the very experiences necessary to develop them (Dalton et al., 2005). Attempts to *train* children in the use of these tools often have limited success, however. In addition to many children finding such an approach stressful in its own right, there is the further problem that many have difficulty generalizing what they have learned in one situation to other situations (Williams White, Koenig, & Scahill, 2007).

Consider, for example, the importance of shared gaze for successful social interaction. It is certainly possible to get a child to attend to someone's eyes to obtain a reward. However, not only may this fail to nurture the child's desire to engage in social interaction, but the meaning of the shared gaze may be lost on the child because his attention is entirely focused on what he must do to obtain the reward (Tantam, 2009). The resulting communicative behaviours are thus immediate and short-term rather than long-term.

A deeper problem concerns the sheer complexity of the myriad nonverbal and verbal signals that a child must deal with in social interactions. Even an apparently straightforward behaviour such as greeting someone is remarkably complex when deconstructed: many subtleties come into play, including who is involved, their relationship to each other, past encounters with the person being greeted, the presence of others, and body language used (McCarthy & Hayes, 1969).

The prospect of trying to instruct children with special needs on all these permutations is daunting. Yet there is cause for optimism that these children can master the subtle nuances of social interaction, and that they can best do so by being encouraged to engage in as wide a variety of social interactions as possible, just like other children (Bruner & Bornstein, 1989). Encouraging them to do so entails

- helping them develop their capacities for self-regulation in all five domains of our model

- recognizing always that the stress load of children with special needs is particularly acute, which predisposes them to *avoid* social interaction

©P

Social Learning and Scaffolding Theory

The primary goal of a social-learning approach is to enhance children's desire and ability to take a willing, active part in social interaction, rather than a passive role in which they are externally conditioned to perform desirable behaviours and avoid undesirable ones. The social-learning approach, especially in the case of children who have special needs, calls for the constant adjustment of scaffolds so that they support basic capacities these children need to become social learners, such as imitating, attending to a caregiver, and directing joint attention to another person or object. The guiding question in such scaffolding should always be: How do we tailor our dealings with the child so that he *wants* to interact?

The biological domain is our best starting point, because we need to mitigate the effects of deficits in this realm, such as hypersensitivity to noise or visual stimuli, that seriously reduce the child's capacity to respond to social overtures. A child with this hypersensitivity is likely to become highly anxious in social situations, which reduces her ability to process social cues. This then not only exacerbates her overall anxiety, but also intensifies her sensitivity to auditory stimuli, setting off a vicious cycle (Loveland, 2005). The reduced capacity to respond adequately in social situations also results in reduced social input (such as other children not wanting to play with the child who is not responding). This constrains the development of specialized brain systems for functions such as understanding the meaning of facial expressions, reading emotions, and the development of functional language skills. This, in turn, seriously limits the child's capacity to engage in interactions and has other measurable effects on all aspects of the child's development (Knudsen, 2004; Lewis, 2005; Mundy & Burnette, 2005). Figure 6.1 gives an overview of the impact of a physiological deficit on a child.

Figure 6.1: Impact of a Physiological Deficit on a Child

None of this is to say that children with special needs have a missing "social-interaction gene" or a defective "mind reading mechanism" that undermines their social-intelligence skills. When such children shy away from social involvement, it is usually due to biological deficits such as the ones noted above, or to serious challenges in emotion regulation. As noted earlier, self-regulation can help to alleviate such problems, and once these children begin to self-regulate, they start to demonstrate both the desire and the ability to engage socially. However, self-regulating for some children can be especially difficult because, as research has shown, in many instances their sensory and discriminatory abilities are hypo- or hyperacute. This means that they often have problems trying to process stimuli that they fail to register, or that they find overwhelming. In many cases the problem is the excessive amount of information that is simply too rapid for them to absorb (Ashwin, Ashwin, Rhydderch, Howells, & Baron-Cohen, 2009). For such children, we have to reduce the demands on their sensory system, strengthen their motor control with carefully structured exercises designed by an occupational therapist, satisfy their needs for certain types of sensory stimulation while helping them avoid other types, and carefully time the presentation of stimuli to meet the child's processing limitations.

The importance of this last point lies in the fact that children who have problems processing dynamic multisensory stimuli have serious difficulties constructing patterns to help them make meaning out of such stimuli. If the presentation of such stimuli is slowed down, however, these difficulties significantly decrease (Gepner & Féron, 2009). Pattern recognition is critical for the speed and efficiency needed to process the rapid, complex onslaught of stimuli involved in most social interactions. The more we can assist a child to acquire these patterns—something that can only be accomplished through numerous exchanges that arise in everyday situations—the more processing capacity is freed up for other aspects of social learning, such as language and social conventions. Without such patterns, the child with special needs is simply overwhelmed by these stimuli, and may resort to repetitive self-calming behaviours such as focusing on spinning objects or his or her fingers, leg bouncing, finger tapping, and pencil twiddling. If excessive, however, these actions may interfere with the child's ability to engage in the very social interactions

 ©P

that are critical for developing the capacity to recognize social patterns in, for example, gestures, facial expressions, and different tones of voice.

Rather than trying to quickly extinguish self-calming behaviours, however, our goal as teachers should be to reduce the stressors causing them—for example, too much noise, overly bright lights, overly exuberant gesturing, or too many people in a room—allowing a student's urge to self-soothe to subside gradually as we help to reorient him or her, through careful scaffolding, toward becoming calm and alert. When you think about it, the preceding can be said about all children. For example, most children are likely to perform better in a test situation when it is administered in a quiet place rather than one with many auditory, visual, and other distractions. For that matter, self-calming behaviours among people in general increase as cognitive, emotional, and social demands on them intensify (Barroso, Freedman, & Grand, 1980). All of us, in fact, benefit when stressors affecting us are reduced and our self-calming is allowed to subside as the calm and focus that come with optimal self-regulation kick in.

This broad understanding of self-calming behaviours leads us to view them not as "abnormal" actions characteristic only of children with special needs, but as ones typical of anyone experiencing increased stress of one kind or another. To be sure, children with special needs are likely to engage in self-calming more frequently and in less socially acceptable ways than typically developing children. Nonetheless, the underlying causes of the self-calming are essentially the same for children with special needs as for typically developing children and the general population.

Therefore, instead of trying to extinguish the self-calming and other behaviours of children that are commonly perceived as problematic, what is required is a scaffolding approach that aims to *decrease* the stress load on these children in the short term, while *increasing* their ability to process larger amounts of information over the long term. Let us look how this approach has unfolded in work being done with children with autism at one centre. It has much to tell us about working with children with special needs in general, both in the classroom and at home.

The Milton & Ethel Harris Research Initiative Treatment (MEHRIT) Program

The Milton & Ethel Harris Research Initiative Treatment (MEHRIT) program has been working with groups of children with autism and their parents. The program is based on Greenspan and Wieder's Developmental Individual Difference Relationship-based (DIR®) model (2008). It is a relational approach, one in which parents meet every other week with a "blended" interdisciplinary team made up of a speech-language pathologist, an occupational therapist, and a mental health specialist, each of them trained in each other's sub-disciplines as well as having received a deeper training in their particular specialty. In these sessions, parents learn techniques for regulating their child and enhancing his or her social development. The goals of these sessions are to

Developmental Individual Difference Relationship-based (DIR®) Model

- identify the stressors on each child and what can be done to reduce them

- help parents understand their child's behaviours (including self-calming and avoidance) and develop strategies for avoiding or dealing with potentially dysregulating experiences

- help the child to cope with a growing range of stressors

- expand the child's emotional range and his or her ability to communicate his or her emotional needs

- enhance the child's desire and ability to interact socially, and to initiate and enjoy such interactions

- enhance his or her capacity to self-regulate

- help parents to become more mindful of their own emotional state and develop strategies for self-regulation

MEHRIT Program

At the beginning of each intervention, each child's parents are asked to agree to the following: in exchange for receiving two hours of therapy for their child every other week (which they attend), as well

©P

as any relevant tests, they will follow the program at home for 20 hours a week and keep logs of these activities. These program activities are characterized by the following key elements:

- There is no use of "artificial motivational reinforcers," such as candies or cookies offered as small rewards to encourage certain behaviours, an approach that has been quite correctly characterized as a "makeshift solution" (Lovaas, 1977). The only incentive for children in the program is the enjoyment of social interactions.

- There are no structured interactions. All interactions are play-based and the focus of each is determined by the child's interest at any given moment, with the therapist following the child's lead. For example, in one situation, a child quickly moved away from playing with a ball and indicated that she would like a cookie from the kitchen. The therapist and parents then encouraged the child to leave the therapy room with them on a "fun visit" to the kitchen, suggesting that she lead the way (thereby developing her sense of agency). They chatted with the child as they did the errand together, helping to make it a social occasion and encouraging the development of her functional communication skills. Though unstructured, these interactions are nonetheless very carefully thought through by the professionals involved.

- Each child's goals are individually determined according to the functional-emotional developmental levels described by Greenspan and Shanker (2004). The goal of therapy for a very low-functioning child, for example, may be to help the child with the ability to attend to her caregiver (see "Functional/Emotional Developmental Levels," below).

Functional/Emotional Developmental Levels

A child goes through four developmental stages as a result of the nurturing interactions experienced with caregivers. Each of these stages continues to develop throughout the child's lifespan. These stages lay the foundation for meaningful language skills and logical reasoning. At each of these stages (for which approximate ages for typically developing children are given below), there is a dominant "structure" for the emotions that guides day-to-day functioning, unites different processing capacities, and orchestrates different parts of the mind and brain.

- Stage 1 (0–3 months) involves becoming calmly focused and alert, a core capacity that will continue to refine and differentiate throughout childhood and adolescence.

- At Stage 2 (2–7 months), we begin to see synchrony in the ways that both the infant and parent use their senses, motor systems, and affective behaviour to connect with each other.

- Stage 3 (3–10 months) is characterized by the development of *intentional* nonverbal communications and gestures, which include facial expressions, arm and leg movements, and vocalizations. At this stage, the infant starts to engage in brief back-and-forth exchanges with her caregiver.

- Stage 4 (9–10 months) involves the child's capacity to engage in a continuous flow of back-and-forth, co-regulated interactions.

Parents play a central role in the intervention for three main reasons:

1. Involvement in activities, both at the therapy sessions and at home, ensures parents' constant engagement in the process.

2. The at-home activities provide essential reinforcement for the work done in the professional therapy sessions, especially with regard to self-regulation, and the skills developed will be functional precisely because they are practised in functional situations.

3. The security and familiarity that the child feels with parents around acts as an important buffer against the anxiety he or she experiences in social interactions.

On average, parents have been doing 26 hours a week on at-home program-related intervention. This is an extraordinary commitment, especially for families already experiencing high levels of stress because of their children's autism. However, you may wonder if such a commitment actually exacerbates the considerable stress these parents are already undergoing. To answer this question, we measure parental stress levels at the beginning, during, and at the end of each year-long intervention. We have found that parents' stress levels rise over the first three months, as they struggle to master the ideas that emerge from their therapy sessions about how to best regulate and engage their child. Then something quite extraordinary happens. Their stress levels begin to drop, and by the end of the intervention, stress levels have dropped quite significantly. Moreover, 94 percent of the families have indicated that they are highly satisfied with the intervention, both for their children and themselves (Mostrangelo, 2010).

Why does this all happen? Probably several factors are involved. One is simply the fact that the children become much better at self-regulation through the combination of the therapy sessions and the parental program-inspired attention at home, as they increasingly engage with their parents and enjoy this involvement. Another factor is the relief that the parents experience when they come to understand why their child behaves in certain ways, what they can do to ease their child's stress, and how they can help their child to avoid stressful situations when possible. In addition, one of our clinicians works closely with parents on their own self-regulation, helping them to understand when and why they are experiencing great stress, which behaviours or situations they find particularly difficult to handle, and how they can best manage those situations and their own level of stress.

Preliminary results of the program (Stieben, Shanker, & Casenhiser, 2012 in prep) show that it has been successfully meeting its goals. Children show greater enjoyment in interactions with their parents, are significantly more cooperative, and take a much more active role in initiating interactions. In short, the interventions are very effectively enabling and motivating children with autism to become calmer and engage in social interactions, thereby setting the stage for the social learning described above.

How then can the approach and results of this initiative help us as teachers to maximize the potential of elementary students with special education needs?

Translating Results into a
Strategy for Special Education

The MEHRIT study represented a unique opportunity to test this therapy model in a controlled laboratory setting. Our challenge now is to translate what we have been learning in a clinical setting into addressing the needs of students with special needs in the classroom. The most important of these lessons is the importance of lowering these students' stress levels by helping them to self-regulate and thereby enhance their capacity for social learning.

As noted at the beginning of this chapter, most of our school systems take a team approach, as the program does, to addressing the kinds of issues that we have been dealing with in our lab. These team approaches should become as "blended" as possible, per the model. The ideas explored in this resource are meant to support the efforts of the teachers, other professionals, and parents who are committed to collaboratively addressing the needs of all children under their care. Addressing these needs, particularly those arising from special needs, can be done in a number of ways, most notably the following:

- Maintaining regular communication among all involved so that adjustments can be made as required, progress tracked, and achievements celebrated.

- Instituting a classroom makeover, such as the one described in Chapter 1 (pp. 11–18), enlisting help as needed.

- Practising the strategies for up- and down-regulating discussed throughout this resource, tailoring them to meet the particular needs of each child.

- Using multimodal assistive learning tools such as those described in Chapter 3 (p. 55). These tools help to spread out the processing load for the child, enabling the use of a sensory strength (e.g., seeing) to scaffold and exercise a sensory weakness (e.g., hearing).

- Using video-call technologies in the classroom such as FaceTime to provide the child with the soothing presence of a parent in situations that the child finds particularly stressful.

©P

Most importantly, remember to always assume that an upward trajectory in learning will continue, no matter how elongated it may be. As long as a child's learning curve is sloping upward, we should never think of that child's level of intelligence as somehow fixed or permanent. An upward trajectory should always give us cause for optimism about the effectiveness of our efforts and the efforts of the child.

What Is "Special" About Special Education?

As important as the research described in this chapter might be for the treatment of children with autism, the implications for special education in general are even greater. If children with autism can learn to master the nuances of social interaction *through* social interaction as they are regulated and learn how to better self-regulate, we have to wonder how many children with special needs can similarly benefit from practices and experiences that enhance their ability to understand and adjust their behaviour to the shifting demands of a classroom. Can the child with a learning disorder learn how to deal with problems that he finds overwhelming by developing strategies to reduce his anxiety? Can the child with ADHD learn to soothe herself, and can the child with an attentional deficit learn to up-regulate himself?

If the answer to all of these questions is "yes," it changes our perception, not just of what a student's customized education plan should look like but, in a sense, of our very understanding of the term *special education*. Perhaps what is most "special" about it is simply the lesson that has been learned from working with the children at our centre: that is, that the more we attempt to teach students with special needs subjects without addressing their self-regulatory issues, the more difficulty they have mastering the material, and the more nonfunctional are the skills or concepts that they acquire. On the other hand, when we work on the roots of their self-regulatory problems, we are helping them to realize their educational potential.

Chapter 7

Self-Regulation and Children's Mental Health

Over the past 25 years, various analyses of population health in Canada have estimated, based on data from the biennial *National Longitudinal Survey of Children and Youth* (Statistics Canada, n.d.) and other sources, that approximately 15 percent of all children and youth (ages 4 to 17) across the country have mental health problems of varying intensity (Offord, Boyle, Fleming, Munroe Blum, & Rae-Grant, 1989; Standing Senate Committee on Social Affairs, Science and Technology, 2004; Waddell, McEwan, Shepherd, Offord, & Hua, 2005; Waddell & Shepherd, 2002; Willms, 2002). One recent study in British Columbia has estimated the rate of vulnerable Kindergarten-aged children in 53 of the province's 59 school districts is 30.3 percent (Human Early Learning Partnership, 2010). (Note that "vulnerable" means these children may experience future challenges in school and in society if they do not receive additional care and support; it does not necessarily mean the children have, or will have, mental health problems.) Also, in some parts of BC, as in the rest of Canada, the statistic for Aboriginal children who are vulnerable is higher still, with a provincial average of 49 percent (Human Early Learning Partnership Aboriginal Steering Committee, 2010).

The most common problems (and some of their manifestations) listed in the above and other related studies are as follows:

- internalizing disorders (e.g., depression, anxiety, phobias, obsessive-compulsive behaviours)

- externalizing disorders (e.g., conduct disorder, oppositional defiance, bullying, vandalism, habitual lying, theft)

- Attention Deficit Hyperactivity Disorder, or ADHD (e.g., a low capacity for paying attention and focusing; fidgeting, restlessness)

- executive function disorders (e.g., significant problems in attentional control or shifting, impulsivity, problems in sequential thinking)

- substance abuse (e.g., addictions to alcohol, smoking, drugs)

- eating disorders (e.g., anorexia, bulimia, food addictions)

- schizophrenia

Needless to say, these problems and their symptoms can be very upsetting in classroom situations, both for the individuals concerned and for teachers and other students. In extreme cases, professionals from outside the school must become involved.

Both the range and prevalence of mental health problems among children and youth should cause us great concern, but we also need to recognize the following issues in the gathering and interpretation of data related to mental health:

- There can be problems in the diagnostic categories and practices used. Clinical assessment often remains more of an art than a science, and there can be inconsistency in the use of diagnostic criteria. In some cases, this can result in misdiagnosis or lack of diagnosis, that is, in incorrectly identifying a disorder or overlooking a disorder altogether (Kirk & Kutchins, 1992).

- There are concerns that anxieties about the possible growth of mental health problems in children may itself contribute to this growth (Kirk & Kutchins, 1992).

- There are problems involved in factoring in co-morbidities. For example, when a child presents both an anxiety disorder and ADHD, this may be recorded as two cases rather than one (Kirk & Kutchins, 1992).

- It is difficult to estimate the percentage of children who might have a disorder but are not seen by medical professionals. A recent study on the prevalence of Autism Spectrum Disorders in a total population sample, for example, suggested that the real incidence rate for these disorders might be even higher than our current estimates of 1.1 percent, which are based solely on medical records (Kim et al., 2011).

This last point raises an important question related to virtually all the mental health problems noted earlier: What about children who have symptoms below a level that would warrant a clinical diagnosis? Can we simply assume that they are "mentally healthy"? Think, for instance, about a child who is getting by in school with mid-range grades, has no close friends, has no interests other than television and video games, is overweight, subdued, anxious, and fearful, but who is not difficult to handle at home or in the classroom. Should we consider such a child to be mentally "just fine"?

What is worrying about the last point above is that it reflects a limited "deficit" view of mental health. According to this view, we do not need to be concerned about a child's mental well-being if that child does not have a disorder as defined by DSM-IV, the *Diagnostic and Statistical Manual of Mental Disorders* (American Psychiatric Association, 2000). This is too restrictive an interpretation of mental health for everyday classroom purposes, however. A much broader view is required.

Encouragingly, such a view is increasingly being reflected in provincial school curricula and related provincial policy documents. For example, in British Columbia's *Health and Career Education K to 7 Integrated Resource Package* (British Columbia Ministry of Education, 2006, p. 248), health is defined comprehensively as

> …physical, social, and emotional (mental) well-being. Optimum health is a state of complete well-being in each dimension, and is not merely the absence of disease or infirmity.

Alberta, in *Positive Futures—Optimizing Mental Health for Alberta's Children and Youth* (Alberta Health and Wellness, 2006, p. 14), subscribes to the definition of mental health from Health and Welfare Canada's 1988 publication *Mental Health for Canadians: Striking a*

©P

Balance, which identifies a key element of mental health as "the optimal development and use…[of] cognitive, affective and relational" abilities. More recently, Ontario's Health and Physical Education curriculum for Grades 1–8 (Ontario Ministry of Education, 2010, p. 213) has reiterated the comprehensive understanding of mental health, while at the same time, as with the BC document, rejecting the deficit view. The Ontario document defines mental health as follows:

> All aspects of a person's well-being that affect his or her emotions, learning, and behaviour. It is important to note that mental health is not merely the absence of mental illness.

S P O T L I G H T

Turning the Table on the Deficit Model of Mental Illness

There is a growing awareness—provincially, nationally, and internationally—that much needs to be done to promote optimal mental health for all people, young and old alike. Health Canada has created The Mental Health Commission of Canada that has, in turn, published *Changing Directions, Changing Lives: The Mental Health Strategy for Canada* (2012). The country's first national strategy on mental health, it is built around these six key elements:

Mental Health Strategies

- promoting mental health and preventing mental illness

- fostering recovery and upholding rights

- providing access to the right services, treatments, and supports

- reducing disparities and addressing diversity

- working with First Nations, Inuit, and Métis

- mobilizing leadership and fostering collaboration

It is telling that in the first paragraph of the document, the authors state that its "release marks a significant milestone in the journey to bring mental health out of the shadows and to recognize, in both words and deeds, the truth of the saying that there can be no health without mental health" (Mental Health Commission of Canada, 2012, p. 6).

Implied in the above statements is the recognition that there are a great number of children who are not actually suffering from clinically identified disorders, but who nonetheless cannot be described as thriving. These children may have little *resiliency*, or "ability to recover quickly from disruptive change, illness or misfortune without being overwhelmed or acting in dysfunctional ways," because they are lacking "the skills to cope with life's challenges" (Ontario Ministry of Children and Youth Services, 2006, p. 25).

This is precisely where self-regulation has such a critical role to play. On the pages that follow, we outline how children cannot thrive, or be resilient, unless they develop the ability to remain calmly focused and alert. While problems with self-regulation cannot be said to *cause* mental health problems, they can exacerbate them. By the same token, the ability to self-regulate contributes significantly to the development of the key attributes of mental health.

Key Attributes of Mental Health

In *The First Idea*, Greenspan and Shanker (2004) define mental health in terms of key attributes, or traits, associated with the development of our capacities as humans to

- feel

- communicate

- relate

- reflect

In this approach, disturbances in mental health are viewed as limitations, to a greater or lesser degree, on the above capacities. For example, the capacity to relate, or form healthy relationships (characterized by warmth, intimacy, stability, and flexibility), is clearly limited for a child who is withdrawn or highly aggressive. In the area of feelings, think of one child's ability to experience, comprehend, and express a range of emotions, and contrast that with another child's capacity to feel only a few, mainly negative, emotions, such as anger and suspicion.

The traits that lead to robust mental health are formed early, encouraged by attentive and nurturing adults, beginning with the child's caregivers and then supplemented by teachers and other professionals. These traits need to be constantly reinforced and broadened, and the earlier we can identify any threats to a child's mental health, the more effectively we can work on minimizing them.

If the mental health policies noted in the introduction of this chapter are to be effective, we have to be very clear about what key attributes characterize a mentally healthy child. Our five-domain model of self-regulation can be very helpful in this regard, as it provides a framework within which to group such attributes. The key attributes of each domain follow.

The Biological Domain: Key Attributes

- Physical health, which includes a robust immune system

- Sufficient energy on waking up, which is maintained through the course of the day

- The ability to recoup energy after difficult experiences

- The ability to remain calm amid distracting visual and auditory stimuli

- The ability to follow healthy daily routines (e.g., healthy diet, sufficient exercise, required hours of sleep)

- Engagement in—and enjoyment of—physical activities, enabled by well-functioning motor systems that, for example, allow the coordination of arms and legs and of eyes and fingers

The Emotional Domain: Key Attributes

- The ability to modulate strong emotions

- Emotional resiliency—the ability to recover from disappointment, challenging situations, embarrassment, and other difficulties, and move forward confidently and positively

- Willingness and interest to experiment and to learn, on one's own and in collaboration with others

- A desire to create and innovate, and while doing so to use a wide range of strategies and techniques
- A healthy self-esteem that is based on awareness of personal efforts and achievements—as well as those of others

The Cognitive Domain: Key Attributes

- The ability to focus, and switch focus, as required
- The ability to consider perspectives other than one's own
- The ability to plan and execute several steps in a row, including being able to try different courses of action when an initial plan has failed to work
- The ability to understand cause and effect
- The ability to think logically
- The ability to set learning goals
- The ability to monitor and assess performance
- The ability to see that failure provides an opportunity to learn
- The ability to manage time effectively
- The ability to develop self-awareness, especially the recognition of personal learning strengths and weaknesses
- The ability to use learning aids, including digital technologies, where appropriate (e.g., making an outline to help order thoughts in writing)

The Social Domain: Key Attributes

- The ability to understand one's feelings and intentions
- The ability to understand the feelings and intentions of others
- The ability to respond to the feelings and intentions of others appropriately, both verbally and nonverbally

- The ability to monitor the effects of one's responses on others

- The ability to be an effective communicator—as a listener and as a speaker

- The ability to demonstrate a good sense of humour that does not rely on ridicule

- The ability to recover from and repair breakdowns in interactions with others (e.g., through compromise)

The Prosocial Domain: Key Attributes

- The ability to help regulate others and to co-regulate with others

- A sense of honesty, both with oneself and with others

- Empathy, or the capacity to care about others' feelings and to help them deal with their emotions

- The ability to put the needs and interests of others ahead of one's own

- The desire to "do the right thing" and the conviction to act on one's convictions

Pathways to Mental Health: Some Case Studies

In the list of attributes in the emotional domain above, as one example, note that recognizing the importance of personal effort in developing the mental health attribute of self-esteem is mentioned. In fact, we need to recognize the importance of effort in developing *all* of these key attributes. Such recognition underscores how critical personal effort is both to mental health and to the self-regulation required to ensure it. Put another way, mental health is very closely tied to self-regulation. To be effective, the latter requires that an individual resolutely and regularly manage threats to his or her well-being through knowing the following issues:

- what circumstances are likely to cause stress and how to prepare for them

- when he or she is experiencing stress

- which stressors he or she finds particularly difficult to handle

- what steps he or she can take to deal with these stressors, including, if necessary, seeking help and accepting it willingly when offered by teachers, parents, and others

The overall goal here is not to remove all stressors from children's lives; this, of course, would be impossible, and it is important to note the beneficial aspects of healthy amounts of stress. Rather, it is to enhance the critical elements identified earlier in this resource (p. xiii) as necessary for optimal self-regulation:

- when feeling calmly focused and alert, the ability to know that one is calm and alert

- when one is stressed, the ability to recognize what is causing the stress

- the ability to recognize stressors both within and outside the classroom

- the desire to deal with those stressors

- the ability to develop strategies for dealing with those stressors

- the ability to recover efficiently and effectively from dealing with stressors

In the context of our discussion here, these are also necessary for the development of a child's overall mental health. As you read through the following three case studies, note how these elements come into play in each instance. Note also

- how teachers, other professionals, children, and parents work collaboratively to achieve the best results

- the scaffolding that takes place as the adults reframe the children's behaviour by nudging them in directions leading to self-regulation

Kids Have Stress Too!®

To help educators' efforts to help their students develop effective stress-management skills, the Psychology Foundation of Canada has developed a series of practical resources for Early Years and Grades 1 to 6 educators.

©P

Ankita

Ankita was a delightful six-year-old in Kindergarten, but she was having a great deal of trouble paying attention to her teacher. She would daydream regularly and sometimes engaged in quiet, private monologues. Her teacher became concerned that such withdrawal behaviour was potentially threatening to Ankita's mental well-being.

The school psychologist agreed this might be the case if the behaviour were to continue. To determine the basis of the problem, he suggested that Ankita might, in fact, have a hearing or comprehension problem. He spoke with Ankita and her parents about this, and they all agreed that she should first have a hearing test. This test established that her hearing was normal, so the psychologist referred her to a speech-language pathologist (SLP). After a session with Ankita, the SLP identified that, while she had a good vocabulary, she was having difficulty with some grammatical constructions, especially prepositions and comparatives. Because of this problem, Ankita would tune out when she could not follow what her teacher was saying.

The SLP began to see Ankita every two weeks, but they made little progress in their sessions, even though they met in a small, quiet room and the therapist would repeat the lessons until she felt that Ankita was using the constructions in question correctly. For example, the therapist would hold up a flash card with a picture of a child sitting on a chair and the word *on* at the top, and another with a child sitting underneath a desk and the word *under* at the top. By the end of such a session, Ankita could use the correct word when she was shown the same card without the word on it. However, at the next session they had to start all over again, working with the same two cards.

Then one day the therapist made a breakthrough. She had brought in exercise balls for Ankita and herself to sit on. At one point, Ankita slipped off her ball. When the therapist asked her if she needed help to get back on, Ankita began to exclaim excitedly, "On! On!" Seizing the moment, the therapist improvised a game in which she crouched underneath a table and beckoned Ankita to join her "under" the table. Then the two of them climbed "into" an open toy chest. In each case, Ankita instantly grasped the meaning of a preposition that, up until then, had been giving her so much trouble.

The therapist immediately abandoned her flash cards. Instead, she began following Ankita's lead, which often afforded an opportunity to work on a particular construction. With a bit of thought and preparation, the therapist was usually able to steer these interactions in a desired direction. For example, bringing a drum and a xylophone into the room one day offered the perfect opportunity to work on the contrasting comparatives *faster/slower* and *louder/softer*. At all times, the therapist was careful not to force the issue: if Ankita decided to go in an entirely different direction, she would follow her lead and seize whatever opportunities for functional language learning emerged. One day, for instance, the teacher brought in a clear plastic container with some toys inside, thinking that they could work on getting the toys *out* of and putting them back *into* the container. Instead, Ankita decided to roll the container on the floor. Following her lead, the therapist switched to a session on *faster* and *slower*.

It soon became clear that a major reason why these sessions were so effective was because the learning was "embodied": that is, Ankita could actually experience the meaning of the word in question, which served to create a very strong emotional connection in her mind between a word and its use (Varela, Thompson, & Rosch, 1992). Another major reason for the effectiveness of this approach was that the movements and activities Ankita was engaging in were helping her to self-regulate, thereby enhancing the ideal state of being calmly focused and alert that best promotes learning, and makes learners such as Ankita feel good about themselves.

Throughout the block of therapy, the SLP was in contact with Ankita's classroom teacher. Having seen the progress that Ankita made in her speech and language, the teacher undertook to learn about embodied cognition so she could better help Ankita to focus and learn in the classroom. It was a clear example for all of the value of multimodal ways of learning.

Tommy

Tommy was nine years old and a challenging Grade 3 student. His main difficulty was dealing with frustration. As soon as he got stuck on a problem, he quickly became angry and would refuse to work on it any longer. No matter how gently or sternly his teacher tried to encourage him to keep at it, these episodes would often end up with Tommy shouting and sometimes even throwing something.

In an interview with his teacher, Tommy's parents revealed that he frequently behaved the same way at home when he got frustrated, and that neither reasoning with nor disciplining him helped calm him. Understandably, they were becoming increasingly concerned about his mental well-being, and asked if he should be seeing the school psychologist. The teacher suggested that might not be necessary, and that she would do her best to deal with the issue in class.

Accordingly, Tommy's teacher worked very hard at scaffolding his frustration problem. She learned that she could minimize the chances of these meltdowns when she raised the bar for him very gradually, making sure to explain any new assignment step by step. She would offer not just verbal praise for his effort, but also tangible rewards, such as being the lunchroom monitor that day—something that he loved—for completing assignments. She also made it clear that there would be consequences for any disruptive behaviour, such as having to stay behind in class during recess to help her tidy up and prepare for the next session.

These scaffolding methods worked well, but only to a point. What the teacher found particularly hard was that often, even when Tommy had mastered a particular kind of problem, and had done so on his own many times, he would suddenly, for no apparent reason, become anxious again. What his teacher came to recognize was that, far from happening for no apparent reason, such behaviour occurred when Tommy was experiencing a particularly high level of stress because of one or more occurrences at home or at school. (His teacher kept in regular contact with his parents to get a good sense of his behaviours at home.)

Sometimes Tommy was stressed because he had not slept enough, because he had not had a good breakfast, or because he had been allowed to play a video game before coming to school that morning. Sometimes it was because of something that happened in the playground before the start of the school day. And sometimes there did not seem to be any reason at all, other than the fact that Tommy had found something very difficult to deal with. Whatever the cause, the key was to reduce Tommy's anxiety and then to teach him ways of doing so on his own to help him feel calm again.

It is also important to note that Tommy's teacher quickly learned that he was upset about his meltdowns, and that what he really wanted were the tools to prevent them from happening. This is reflected in the following exchange between the two one day, as the teacher tries to lead him gently out of his upset state toward an activity in which he will have a good chance to self-regulate:

> **Teacher** (speaking gently): Tommy, please try to calm down and tell me why you're so upset.
>
> **Tommy** (shouting): I want to calm down, but I can't!
>
> **Teacher** (in a soothing voice): OK, OK, but please stop shouting and try to tell me quietly what's bothering you.
>
> **Tommy** (more calmly): I'm feeling real tired, and I can't solve this math problem. I hate subtraction!
>
> **Teacher:** Well, how about trying to use these blocks to figure out how much 21 minus 15 is? Remember how you tried that the other day and these blocks made it so much easier for you?
>
> **Tommy** (somewhat grudgingly): OK, I'll try that again.
>
> **Teacher:** That's great! Here you go.

The teacher then placed 21 blocks in front of Tommy on the table, and he saw that there were 6 blocks left when he moved 15 of them to one side. He looked pleased about this and proceeded to give his teacher the right answer.

> **Teacher:** That's terrific! Now do you want to try another problem with the blocks, or do you want to try one without them?
>
> **Tommy** (much calmer now): Let me try one without the blocks.

Notice how Tommy's anxiety begins to diminish as soon as he starts working both physically and cognitively on the problem. Moving the blocks around has a regulating effect on him, as does the feel of the soft wood of the blocks on his fingers. After successfully completing this problem with the blocks, Tommy did a second subtraction problem without using them. He solved this problem as well, and clearly enjoyed the experience of doing so.

RJ

RJ came in to MEHRI with his parents when he was in Grade 5, ostensibly because he was getting poor grades, but really because his parents were concerned about his mental health. As soon as he entered our offices, we noticed that he was overweight and very subdued. Despite our best efforts to get him to smile, RJ remained poker-faced. The only time he became animated was when we asked him to tell us about his friends. He said that his best friend was "Crusher," who lived far away, in Australia. He followed this up with a catalogue of his other "friends" around the world, all members, it turned out, of an online gaming community. In other words, RJ had no real friends.

RJ had flown under the radar for years, mainly because, as his mother put it, "he is the easiest of my four children to handle, and his teachers say he's easy to manage in class." RJ's parents were warm but overindulgent. They made few demands on RJ, and rarely threatened to punish him—and when they *did* threaten, they would never follow through. They exerted little control over his daily activities and, indeed, permitted him to make decisions about such things as when he would go to bed, how much television he would watch, and when or what he would eat.

One particularly telling thing that we noticed on his first visit was how, when RJ went to lower himself in a chair that had no arms on it, he clumsily collapsed when he was a few centimetres from the seat. This, we realized, might be a sign that he was having trouble coping with and integrating the quantity of information his nervous system was taking in through his limbs, muscles, and joints about the position and movement of his body (the problem of *sensory integration*, mentioned earlier in Chapter 1, p. 6).

For a child with this problem of overload and integration, even routine physical activities such as sitting—especially for long periods of time such as at a classroom desk—can be very demanding and dysregulating. If this problem is not addressed, the child may increasingly retreat into an isolated and isolating world that is potentially threatening to his mental well-being. In RJ's case, he avoided all forms of sport and even just playing with other children. Instead, he constantly played video games, which provided his nervous system with continuous electronic stimulation.

RJ's mother reported that he was "in another world" when playing his online games, which made it almost impossible to get his attention. Our concern here was that the techniques of "attentional capture"—the frenetic barrage of rapidly changing images, loud noises, bright colours, and the like, deployed by these games—were further draining RJ's energy reserves by providing brief but exhausting jolts of energy that further dysregulated him. Their effect was essentially the same as that provided by the high-energy, high-fat content of fast, or "junk," foods that, we were not surprised to learn, were also a favourite of RJ's (see "The False, Exhausting Energy of Fast Foods," below).

S P O T L I G H T

The False, Exhausting Energy of Fast Foods

In *The Surgeon General's Vision for a Healthy and Fit Nation* (2010), the Surgeon General of the United States, Regina Benjamin, lists the primary reasons why the consumption of fast foods has become such a cause of great concern. In addition to the dangers of eating high-density caloric foods, she cites the dangerous consumption of high-fructose drinks (which has been related to both the obesity epidemic and a dental epidemic in children). Also of concern are the use of food additives, the dangers of caffeinated soft drinks, and the overconsumption of candy. All of these foods are addictive, leading to a rapid release of energy followed by its quick and sharp decline (Taubes, 2007).

Recent data indicates that there has been a dramatic increase in the number of calories that children consume daily, and that 50 percent of these calories come from consuming fats and sugars (Nestle, 2007). These trends have prompted warnings that, because of unhealthy eating habits and physical inactivity, the present generation of children may be the first to have a shorter life expectancy than their parents (Carmona, 2004).

RJ's consumption of such foods—including ice cream, candy, doughnuts, chips, and soft drinks in particular—was not simply the cause but also the *consequence* of his self-regulatory problems. That is, faced with chronic energy depletion from his poor gross-motor control and his constant video-gaming, RJ turned to sources of fast-energy release. Moreover, his parents frequently offered him junk food as an incentive to secure compliance, or sometimes simply just to get him to eat something.

Added to all this, not surprisingly, was the shame of being overweight and generally clumsy (as we had seen when he first tried to sit down in our office). In fact, RJ's one source of positive self-esteem was coming from his online game activities: he was a leading scorer in these games, a fact that was broadcast on his favourite gaming website and earned him admiring emails from other gamers.

We decided that the key to encouraging RJ to self-regulate and thereby enhance his general mental health was not to impose a sudden and jarring change to his day-to-day routine. Rather, we first advised his teacher to try fidget toys, a technique that was mentioned in Chapter 1 (p. 15). We suggested this because it struck us that the finger tapping involved in playing video games might be serving a bit of a self-regulating function, much like jiggling, so we gave him some fidget toys to play with on his desk. His favourite was playdough, which he would mould and remould constantly, seemingly unaware that he was doing so.

The next thing we addressed was the need for RJ to move more, as he was so accustomed to sitting mesmerized and still while playing his video games. We arranged to get a swivel chair for him in his classroom, one that he could raise and lower as well as shift around in. Sure enough, he was constantly making small movements in this chair, something that clearly helped him to self-regulate, as shown in a slow but steady increase in his alertness in class.

While these techniques were met with some success, a meeting of RJ's teacher and parents concluded that where he needed help the most was in the social domain. His teacher suggested that the perfect opportunity to do this existed in the community: a video game club, one of many different clubs offered at a long-established local after-four program, located just around the corner from the school. The club was part of an overall program for children and youth. The gaming club provided the opportunity for RJ to venture into a social setting that was very much based in his comfort zone—video gaming. Each session at the club would begin with a group conversation. At the first session, the counsellor had the children talk a little about themselves: what they liked doing and what they wanted to be when they grew up. He worked hard to create an atmosphere of shared respect and mutual trust among the children and himself.

For the first few weeks, most of each session was spent playing some chosen video game. The allure of the centre was that there were a host of clubs and activities the children could join, all on a voluntary basis. The counsellor encouraged the children to use some of the other resources of the centre, which included a dance studio, a full gym, a pool, and a music studio. RJ, along with a few of his video-gaming friends, decided to try floor hockey one night. He had a lot of trouble keeping the ball on his stick and shooting accurately, but so did a number of other children. As it turned out, everyone had a good time, and when it was time to stop, RJ was shouting as loud as all the other kids for "just five more minutes."

For RJ, as for so many children who are overstressed, a critical step toward better mental health is the experience of interacting with peers, some of whom may be struggling with similar issues. In this inclusive social environment, RJ found that it was safe to begin to open up about the things that were bothering him with the counsellor, but also to develop new interests such as floor hockey and the centre's music studio. Instead of further depleting his energy reserves, these activities re-energized him and helped him to self-regulate and feel better about himself.

Over the course of the year, RJ did, in fact, begin to lose weight as a consequence of increased physical activity, better eating habits, more time spent playing with friends, and much less time spent playing video games. The most significant change of all occurred when that poker-faced kid we first met was replaced by a smiling, happy 11 year old.

The Mental Well-Being of Teachers

What about the mental well-being of teachers themselves? Let's begin by recalling a statement made by Kyle, the Grade 6 teacher we met in Chapter 2:

> …whenever a child became angry, a sort of cold feeling seemed to take over me and, before I knew it, I was responding angrily myself. Now I find that I can remain just as calm in the face of their anger as around all their other emotions.

This statement is instructive because it reminds us that as teachers we need to attend not only to our students' academic and psychological needs, but also to our own mental health as we try our best every day to keep up with and implement curriculum, assess students, deal with parents, and fulfill many other duties. All this, as no doubt your daily experiences and recent studies attest, is extremely demanding.

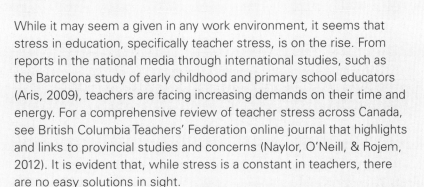

S P O T L I G H T

Studies on Teachers' Mental Well-Being

The challenges of facing a classroom of children trying to cope with a variety of academic and psychological issues can be very taxing for teachers and a challenge to their own capacity to self-regulate. Numerous studies on teacher burnout in recent years have indicated that, in many cases, both early retirees and those leaving teaching are doing so for stress-related reasons (Clark & Antonelli, 2009; Lambert & McCarthy, 2006; Coulter & Abney, 2009; Webb, Frampton, Henderson, & Hyman, 2009).

While it may seem a given in any work environment, it seems that stress in education, specifically teacher stress, is on the rise. From reports in the national media through international studies, such as the Barcelona study of early childhood and primary school educators (Aris, 2009), teachers are facing increasing demands on their time and energy. For a comprehensive review of teacher stress across Canada, see British Columbia Teachers' Federation online journal that highlights and links to provincial studies and concerns (Naylor, O'Neill, & Rojem, 2012). It is evident that, while stress is a constant in teachers, there are no easy solutions in sight.

Teacher Burnout

The second sentence in Kyle's statement also points to something that can help teachers maintain their equilibrium. It suggests that teachers themselves need to do what this resource encourages them to have their students do: self-regulate. Might some of the techniques for developing self-regulation in children that you have read about in this resource be effective in some form for teachers as well? A recent pilot project in New Zealand has a lot to tell us in this regard.

The Rangi Ruru Pilot Project for Teachers

Rangi Ruru Early Childhood College is located in Christchurch, New Zealand. Several years ago, a teacher there named Norah invited me to help with a pilot project for teachers based on what she had read about our work on self-regulation. She was particularly intrigued by our work with parents, and thought that it was transferable to teachers to help them with their own self-regulation and mental well-being.

I agreed to help Norah set up a project at Rangi Ruru with the following two main outcomes:

1. to steer teachers away from behaviour-management techniques that try to extinguish or curtail troubling behaviours in children, and instead steer them toward understanding the root causes of such behaviour, thereby helping the teachers address problems in their students' self-regulation within the framework of the five-domain model

2. to enhance the teachers' own capacity to self-regulate as they became more effective at dealing with their students' problems— by providing them with the techniques to do so

Norah's message to the teachers on the first day of classes was this: the project would offer them the opportunity to look closely at a domain of their choosing through the lens of self-regulation as it applied to both their students and to themselves. First, though, they would be given a solid grounding in the biological domain, that of arousal regulation, which meant covering the topics discussed in Chapter 1.

Whatever domains the teachers chose to investigate, we guided their reading and responded to their questions. Norah made it clear to the Rangi Ruru teachers from the start that they would be challenged in whatever domain they chose to research. We expected them to read and absorb related academic papers such as the ones listed in the References of this resource (see pp. 161–174), and to work with others who had chosen the same domain in order to make collaborative presentations on their findings. They would also be required to write individual reflective essays on how what they had

 ©P

learned was changing the way they worked with their students and helping them to maintain their own equilibrium in the classroom.

Norah emphasized that she would be there to support them at all times in whatever way she could as they explored what was new and exciting territory for them. Essentially, we wanted them to learn as much as they could about our current state of knowledge concerning the factors that contribute to problems in self-regulation, as well as about what they could do in the classroom to enhance both their students' and their own capacity to self-regulate. For the teacher-related part of this second main outcome, the goals were to help the teachers

- understand what student behaviours and what classroom situations they found particularly challenging, and why

- recognize when they were themselves overstressed and dysregulated, and what they needed to do to up- or down-regulate themselves in order to cope with strong emotions in a student, such as anger, anxiety, and frustration

It was instructive for each of them, not to mention for Norah and myself, to see how often the teachers interpreted their inability to manage a student as somehow reflecting their own shortcomings as a teacher. What was particularly interesting was how they found different behaviours or situations particularly difficult and potentially (if not actually) dysregulating for themselves. For some, it was students yelling, for others it was when a student was withdrawn or sulky, or overexcited, or when they could not engage a student. A few teachers found parent interviews difficult to handle—one even mentioned not being able to sleep the night before these took place.

Ultimately, we wanted the Rangi Ruru teachers to be able to understand and address the needs of the children they were teaching, but to do so while acknowledging their own needs so they could cope with—and thrive in the face of—the daily challenges of the classroom. For some, it was taking a walk during lunch hour or talking to colleagues about something that was troubling them. One group organized a before-school walk, another an after-school exercise session. Some found brief conversations with Norah or email exchanges with me in faraway Canada helpful.

The essay assignment, in particular, resulted in thoughtful and enthusiastic accounts of how the lens of self-regulation had changed each teacher's perception of particular students and classroom situations. In the essays, we read inspiring descriptions about the effects of the project on the teachers' views about the importance and rewards of teaching and on their overall sense of mental well-being.

One teacher, for example, wrote a description of a five-year-old child who had been acting up in class. Instead of becoming annoyed, she asked the student if he would like to go outside for a break with an educational assistant. The child headed straight for the swings, and the teacher suddenly realized, from her recent reading on how swinging calms some children with balance problems, that this child seemed to spend every moment he could on the swings during recess. From her vantage point she could see, almost from the first moment the child started swinging, how his face relaxed and he began to smile. When he returned to the classroom she asked him what it was that he found so hard there and if the swings always made him feel better. After a few minutes, the child started to open up and he told her that the other kids were way too noisy and that when they started shouting he always felt as if his muscles were going to explode (a sensation caused by a buildup of adrenalin). As soon as he started swinging, however, that feeling would go away. The teacher's concluding words about this episode were typical of statements made in all the essays:

> For me it came as a revelation that this child's behaviour in class was like a warning light going on, telling me that I had to explore what was really going on inside this little boy. I came to realize just what an important role I was playing in his future. As soon as I thought this, I realized that exactly the same change in mood that I had seen in this child was happening to me. I was suddenly relaxing and feeling much less anxious about this child. What really brought the whole lesson home was when the EA asked me what I was smiling about.

©P

Concluding Words and Looking Ahead

This final section would really have been much more aptly entitled "Beginning," for that is how we view this resource. As we made clear in the Introduction, our primary goal is to help students achieve optimal self-regulation. Developmental psychologists and psychophysiologists (those studying the interrelationships between the mind and the body's physical response) have been studying self-regulation intently for the past two decades. Over a similar period, much work has been done on self-regulated learning in Canada and elsewhere (see Butler, 2011; Whitebread, Bingham, Grau, Pino Pasternak, & Sangster, 2007; Zimmerman & Schunk, 2012). In fact, Canada has emerged as one of the world's leading centres for research on self-regulated learning (see Alexander & Winne, 2006; Muis, 2007; Perry & Rahim, 2011; Winne, 2005; Woolfolk, Winne, & Perry, 2009). Our hope is that the material presented in this resource will be seen as a bridge between these fields of research on self-regulation and, indeed, as strengthening the foundation for this exciting area of educational psychology.

We will continue to see important advances in our understanding of the very nature of self-regulation (see any of the papers by Clancy Blair, beginning with Blair, 2002); the neuroscience of self-regulation (see any of the papers by Adele Diamond, beginning with Diamond & Lee, 2011); the neurobiology of self-regulation (see Diamond, 2002;

Lewis, 2011); and the psychophysiology of self-regulation (see Porges, 2011). We will also begin to learn more about the reasons why children might experience difficulty in one or more of the domains surveyed—and effective practices for addressing these challenges. No doubt, over time, our five-domain model will be significantly modified and improved. We welcome these changes.

In other words, the goal of those of us who worked on this resource, and that of the clinical and scientific team at MEHRI, was to build on Stanley Greenspan's vision of a new lens for viewing children's behaviour: a new way of thinking about the reasons why children might be having trouble controlling their impulses or focusing their attention, and what we as educators can do about it. This new lens is intended to supplant the behaviourist outlook that has had such a strong influence on educational thinking for the past 50 years.

That is not to say that behaviourism was somehow misguided; how could a scientific analysis of behaviour ever be "wrong"? Maybe a particular study was not rigorous enough or should have looked more carefully at intervening variables. But correlations are correlations, and when they are strong they are important.

Yet beginning in the late 1970s, Greenspan began to worry that the behaviourist paradigm had a number of limitations (Greenspan, 1979). For one thing, what were assumed would be fairly straightforward correlations between behaviours and outcomes were far more complex than had been expected. Certain kinds of behaviours are less persistent than had been assumed; and the relationship between specific behaviours and educational outcomes turns out to be highly variable and influenced by myriad factors.

Equally worrying was the fact that our efforts to change particular behaviours in the classroom were turning out to be somewhat hit-or-miss. It seemed clear that certain behaviours (such as aggression) appear early and are strong predictors of downstream educational problems; yet these behaviours are highly resistant to intervention. In the case of those behaviours that do seem amenable to change (for example, compliance), the improvements observed seem to have more to do with the bond formed between teacher and child than the actual intervention method employed.

Moreover, managing a child's behaviour—especially when one is dealing with a group of children in which a significant number are

©P

experiencing difficulties with learning—is incredibly draining. It seemed so straightforward when the founders of behaviourism described how one could manage any behaviour by sticking to a conditioning protocol; but, in classroom practice, genuine change is remarkably difficult to achieve or sustain and, in some cases (for example, when dealing with aggression), the intervention actually seems to make the behaviour worse for a significant number of children.

Even more worrying is that the number of children exhibiting various sorts of unproductive behaviours seems to have been growing at an exponential rate over the past decade. The fact is that the educational system, already straining at the seams, is facing a dramatic increase in the severity of problematic behaviours, and a relentless increase in the number of children needing attention (see Angus et al., 2009).

But perhaps the greatest problem with operating at the level of "behaviour" is that it is difficult to explain why we see certain clusters. In 2006, Fraser Mustard identified the striking convergence over a lifespan between problems in mental health, physical health, and educational outcomes. But why should this be the case? Why should aggression or inattentiveness be such a strong predictor of, as examples, vulnerability to risky behaviours, cardiovascular disease, and poor literacy? This was a question that behaviourism was poorly equipped to answer.

Early Child Development and Experience-Based Brain Development

The inspiration for the self-regulation framework presented in this resource, therefore, was the need to

- understand the underlying *causes* of behaviours

- understand *why* behaviours should be tied to a fixed outcome

- survey types of activities and practices intended to address the underlying causes of behaviours

- explore the links between mental health, physical health, and education in terms of the underlying causes of behaviours

At still a deeper level, however, the inspiration for this resource was to highlight the importance of universal education for the well-being of society. Throughout Canada, we have seen a rapidly growing awareness of the wisdom of investing in the early years. But it is vital to recognize, first, that many children might not have access to early years resources; second, that it can take many years to help a child truly learn how to self-regulate; and third, that some children might suffer "regressions" because of some highly stressful event in their lives.

The fact is that early school leaving, suspension, and worst of all, expulsion, are glaring signs of our failure as a society, not that of our children. The challenges that we face in our national dream of seeing every child graduate and go on to lead a rich and rewarding life are daunting. Our hope is that this resource might contribute to the efforts being made to promote student self-regulation and bring our dream a step closer to reality.

©P

A

Adrenaline—the hormone involved in acceleration

Affect Signals—non-verbal means we use to indicate our emotions or mood, including tone of voice, gestures, and facial expressions (such as a smile or annoyed look)

Attention Deficit Hyperactivity Disorder (ADHD)—a chronic condition affecting 7 to 12 percent of children. It includes a combination of problems, e.g., difficulty sustaining attention, hyperactivity, and impulsive behaviour. Children with ADHD often struggle with self-esteem, relationships, and performance in school. (ADD, an older term, describes children who are not hyperactive but have difficulty focusing.)

Auditory Processing—the ability to distinguish between similar sounds and words, separate speech from background noise, and recall and comprehend what was heard

Autonomic Nervous System—the system that controls many organs and muscles within our body. It is divided into two parts: the sympathetic nervous system and parasympathetic nervous system.

B

Bullying—physical, verbal, or mental abuse directed at one or more individuals, usually repeatedly, and intended to harm

C

Co-regulation—a process in which two individuals observe and understand each other and adjust their behaviour to help each other reach optimal levels of regulation

Cortisol—the hormone involved in slowing down to a condition of rest

D

Downstream—happening at a later stage

Dysregulation—an impairment or interruption of a regulatory system that interferes with a child's ability to regulate him- or herself in a domain

E

Executive Functions—cognitive processes that regulate areas such as planning, working memory, problem solving, mental flexibility, and multi-tasking

M

Metacognition—the awareness and understanding of one's own thinking or cognitive processes

P

Parasympathetic Nervous System (PNS, occasionally PSNS)—the system for recovery or slowing down to a condition of rest. PNS can refer to the peripheral nervous system (the nerves and ganglia outside of the brain and spinal cord) and the parasympathetic nervous system. An online search for PNS usually results in the former.

Proprioceptor—a sensory receptor found in muscles, tendons, joints, and the inner ear, which responds to position and movement

S

Sympathetic Nervous System (SNS)—the system for acceleration that results in quick action

ACT for Youth. (2002, May). Adolescent brain development. In *Research facts and findings*. Retrieved June 15, 2012, from http://www.actforyouth.net/resources/rf/rf_brain_0502.cfm

Alberta Education. (2005). *Heart of the matter: Character and citizenship education initiative*. Edmonton, AB: Alberta Education.

Alberta Education. (2011). Competencies for 21st century learning. In *AISI: Improving Student Learning*. Retrieved July 1, 2012, from http://education.alberta.ca/admin/aisi/themes/21-century.aspx

Alberta Health and Wellness. (2006). *Futures—Optimizing mental health for Alberta's children and youth: A framework for action 2006–2016*. Edmonton, AB: Alberta Health and Wellness.

Alexander, P. A., & Winne, P. H. (2006). Afterword. In P. A. Alexander & P. H. Winne (Eds.). *Handbook of educational psychology* (2nd ed., pp. 981–984). Mahwah, NJ: Lawrence Erlbaum.

American Psychiatric Association. (2000). *Diagnostic and statistical manual of mental disorders* (4th ed.). Washington, DC: American Psychiatric Publications.

Angus, M., McDonald, T., Ormond, C., Rybarczyk, R., Taylor, A., & Winterton, A. (2009). *Trajectories of classroom behaviour and academic progress: A study of student engagement with learning*. Perth, Australia: Edith Cowan University.

Aris, N. (2009). Burnout syndrome in educators. *Electronic Journal of Research in Educational Psychology, 7*(2), 829–848.

Ashwin, E., Ashwin, C., Rhydderch, D., Howells, J., & Baron-Cohen, S. (2009, January). Eagle-eyed visual acuity: An experimental investigation of enhanced perception in autism. *Biological Psychiatry, 65*(1), 17–21.

Bandura, A. (1977). *Social learning theory*. New York, NY: General Learning Press.

Bar-On, R. (2005). The Bar-On model of emotional-social intelligence (ESI). Retrieved June 26, 2012, from http://www.ressourcesetmanagement.com/Article%20prof%20%20Baron%20.pdf

Barroso, F., Freedman, N., & Grand, S. (1980). Self-touching performance and attentional processes. *Perceptual and Motor Skills, 50*(3, Pt. 2), 1083–1089.

Baumeister, R. F. (2002). Ego depletion and self-control failure: An energy model of the self's executive function. *Self and Identity, 1*, 129–136.

Baumeister, R. F., & Leary, M. R. (2005). The need to belong: Desire for interpersonal attachments as a fundamental human motivation. *Psychological Bulletin, 117*(3), 497–529.

Baumeister, R. F., & Vohs, K. D. (Eds.). (2011). *Handbook of self-regulation: Research, theory, and applications* (2nd ed). New York, NY: Guilford Press.

Beebe, B., & Lachmann, F. M. (1998). Co-constructing inner and relational processes: Self- and mutual regulation in infant research and adult treatment. Retrieved June 25, 2012, from New York State Psychiatric Institute website: http://www.nyspi.org/Communication_Sciences/PDF/Infant%20 research%20and%20adult%20treatment/BB-co-constructing%20inner%20 and%20relational%203.6.07.pdf

Bekoff, M. (1999, March 11). Mark Bekoff—Animal behavior and emotions [Video file]. Retrieved June 27, 2012, from http://www.youtube.com/ watch?v=HOWnXJW9LjI

Bekoff, M. (2011). Animal emotions. *Psychology Today*. Retrieved from http:// www.psychologytoday.com/blog/animal-emotions

Bendixen, A., Grimm, S., Deouell, L. Y., Wetzel, N., Mädebach, A., & Schröger, E. (2010). The time-course of auditory and visual distraction effects in a new crossmodal paradigm. *Neuropsychologia*, *48*(7), 2130–2139.

Berk, L. E., Mann, T. D., & Ogan, A. T. (2006). Make believe play: Wellspring for development of self-regulation. In D. G. Singer, R. M. Golinkoff, & K. Hirsh-Pasek (Eds.), *Play=Learning: How play motivates and enhances children's cognitive and social-emotional growth.* New York, NY: Oxford University Press.

Berkowitz, M.W. (1998). The education of the complete moral person. In Studies in Social and Moral Development and Education [Website]. Retrieved June 28, 2012, from http://tigger.uic.edu/~lnucci/MoralEd/ articles/berkowitzed.html

Biederman, I., & Vessel, E. A. (2006). Perceptual pleasure and the brain. *American Scientist, 94*, 25.

Blackburn, R. (1993). *The psychology of criminal conduct: Theory, research and practice.* Toronto, ON: John Wiley & Sons.

Blair, C. (2002). School readiness: Integrating cognition and emotion in a neurobiological conceptualization of children's functioning at school entry. *American Psychologist, 57*(2): 111–127.

Blair, C., & Diamond, A. (2008). Biological processes in prevention and intervention: The promotion of self-regulation as a means of preventing school failure. *Development and Psychopathology*, *20*(03), 899–911.

Bobbio, T, Gabbard, C., & Caçola, P. (2009). Interlimb coordination: An important facet of gross-motor ability. *Early Childhood Research & Practice, 11*(2). Retrieved July 16, 2012, from http://ecrp.uiuc.edu/v11n2/bobbio.html

Boekaerts, M., & Corno, L. (2005). Self-regulation in the classroom: A perspective on assessment and intervention. *Applied Psychology: An International Review*, *54*(2), 199–231.

Boersma, S. N., & Maes, S. (2006). Psychological consequences of myocardial infarction: A self-regulation perspective on health-related quality of life and cardiac rehabilitation. *Netherlands Heart Journal*, *14*(10), 335–338.

©P

Bradley, S. J. (2000). *Affect Regulation and the Development of Psychopathology.* New York, NY: Guilford Press.

British Columbia Ministry of Education. (2006). *Health and career education K to 7 integrated resource package.* Victoria, BC: Ministry of Education.

Brophy, J., Alleman, J., & Knighton, B. (2010). *A learning community in the primary classroom.* New York, NY: Routledge.

Bruner, J. (1977). *The process of education.* Cambridge, MA: Harvard University Press.

Bruner, J. (1983). *Child's talk: Learning to use language.* New York, NY: W. W. Norton & Company.

Bruner, J. (1985). Vygotsky: An historical and conceptual perspective. In J. V. Wertsch (Ed.), *Culture, communication, and cognition: Vygotskian perspectives* (pp. 21–34). London, UK: Cambridge University Press.

Bruner, J., & Bornstein, M. (1989). On interaction. In M. Bornstein & J. Bruner (Eds.), *Interaction in human development* (pp. 199–220). Hillsdale, NJ: Lawrence Earlbaum.

Budiansky, S. (2003). *The character of cats: The origins, intelligence, behavior, and stratagems of* Felis silvestris catus. New York, NY: Penguin.

Butler, D. L. (2011). Investigating self-regulated learning using in-depth case studies. In B. J. Zimmerman & D. H. Schunk (Eds.), *Handbook of self-regulation of learning and performance* (pp. 346–360). New York, NY: Routledge.

Canadian Safe School Network. (n.d.). SNAP steps. Retrieved June 15, 2012, from http://www.canadiansafeschools.com/programs/programs/SNAP/SNAPsteps.htm

Carmona, R. H. (2004, March 2). The growing epidemic of childhood obesity. Testimony of the US Surgeon General before the Subcommittee on Competition, Infrastructure, and Foreign Commerce Committee on Commerce, Science, and Transportation, United States Senate. Retrieved July 2, 2012, from http://www.surgeongeneral.gov/news/testimony/childobesity03022004.html

Casenhiser, D. M., Shanker, S. G., & Stieben, J. (2011). Learning through interaction in children with autism: Preliminary data from a social-communication-based intervention. *Autism.* Prepublished September 26, 2011 DOI: 10.1177/1362361311422052

Clark, R., & Antonelli, F. (2009). *Why teachers leave: Results of an Ontario survey, 2006–08.* Toronto, ON: Ministry of Education.

Cleary, B. (1990). *The mouse and the motorcycle.* New York, NY: HarperCollins.

Cohen, E. G. (1994). Restructuring the classroom: Conditions for productive small groups. *Review of Educational Research, 64,* 1–35.

Committee for Children. (2005). *Steps to Respect program guide: A review of research.* Retrieved June 27, 2012, from http://www.cfchildren.org/Portals/0/STR/STR_DOC/Research_Review_STR.pdf

Coulter, M. A., & Abney, P. C. (2009). A Study of burnout in international and country of origin teachers. *International Review of Education, 55*(1), 105–121.

Crockett, L. J., Raffaelli, M., & Shen Y-H. (2006). Linking self-regulation and risk proneness to risky sexual behavior: Pathways through peer pressure and early substance use. *Journal of Research on Adolescence, 16*(4), 503–525.

Dalton, K. M., Nacewicz, B. M., Johnstone, T., Schaefer, H. S., Gernsbacker, M. A., Goldsmith, H. H., Alexander, A. L., & Davidson, R. J. (2005, April). Gaze fixation and the neural circuitry of face processing in autism. *Natural Neuroscience, 8*(4), 519–526.

DanceDance Revolution. (2011, November 16). [Video game]. Tokyo, Japan, Konami.

Deci, E. L., Koestner, R., & Ryan, R. M. A. (1999). Meta-analytic review of experiments examining the effects of extrinsic rewards on intrinsic motivation. *Psychological Bulletin, 125*(6), 627–668.

de Waal, F. B. M. (Ed.). (2002). *Tree of origin: What primate behavior can tell us about human evolution.* Cambridge, MA: Harvard University Press.

de Waal, F. B. M. (2009). *The age of empathy: Nature's lessons for a kinder society.* New York, NY: Crown Publishing Group.

Dewar, G. (2009). Teaching empathy: Evidence-based tips for fostering empathy in children. Retrieved June 27, 2012, from http://www.parentingscience.com/teaching-empathy-tips.html

Diamond, A. (2002). Normal development of prefrontal cortex from birth to young adulthood: Cognitive functions, anatomy, and biochemistry. In D. T. Stuss & R. T. Knight (Eds.), *Principles of frontal lobe function* (pp. 466–503). London, UK: Oxford University Press.

Diamond, A., & Lee, K. (2011). Interventions shown to aid executive function development in children 4 to 12 years old. *Science, 333* (6045), 959–964.

Doidge, N. (2007). *The brain that changes itself: Stories of personal triumph from the frontiers of brain science.* New York, NY: Penguin Group.

Duckworth, A. L., & Seligman, M. E. P. (2005). Self-discipline outdoes IQ in predicting academic performance of adolescents. *Psychological Science, 16*(2), 939–944.

Dugatkin, L. A. (2006). *The altruism equation.* Princeton, NJ: Princeton University Press.

Durlak, J. A., Weissberg, R. P., Dymnicki, A. B., Taylor, R. D., & Schellinger, K. B. (2011). The impact of enhancing students' social and emotional learning: A meta-analysis of school-based universal interventions. *Child Development, 82*(1), 405–432.

Eisenberg, N., Fabes, R. A., Schaller, M., Miller, P., Carlo, G., Poulin, R., Shea, C., & Shell, R. (1991). Personality and socialization correlates of vicarious emotional responding. *Journal of Personality and Social Psychology, 61,* 459–470.

Eisenberg, N., & Mussen, P. H. (1989). *The roots of prosocial behavior in children.* Cambridge, UK: Cambridge University Press.

Eisenberg, N., Smith, C., & Spinrad, T. L. (2011). Effortful control: Relations with emotion regulation, adjustment, and socialization in childhood. In R. F. Baumeister & K. D. Vohs (Eds.), *Handbook of self-regulation: Research, theory, and applications* (pp. 263–283). New York, NY: Guilford Press.

Ekman, P., & Friesen, W. V. (2003). *Unmasking the face: A guide to recognizing emotions from facial expressions.* Cambridge, MA: Malor Books.

Eysenck, H. J., & Eyesenck, M. W. (1985). *Personality and individual differences: A natural science approach.* New York, NY: Plenum Press.

FABtale. (2009). [Software]. Australia: FABTale Productions.

Flavell, J. H. (1979). Metacognition and cognitive monitoring: A new area of cognitive-developmental inquiry. *American Psychologist 34*(10), 906–911.

Fogel, A. (2009). *The psychophysiology of self-awareness: Rediscovering the lost art of body sense.* New York, NY: W. W. Norton.

Galton, M., & MacBeath, J. (2008). *Teachers under pressure.* London, UK: SAGE Publications.

Gardner, H. (1983). *Frames of mind: The theory of multiple intelligences.* New York, NY: Basic Books.

Gepner, B., & Féron, F. (2009). Autism: A world changing too fast for a mis-wired brain? *Neuroscience and Biobehavioral Reviews, 33,* 1227–1247.

Gladwell, M. (2008). *Outliers: The story of success.* New York, NY: Little, Brown & Company.

Goleman, D. (2006). *Social intelligence: The new science of human relationships.* New York, NY: Bantam.

Gonzalez-Lima, F., & Scheich, H. (1985). Ascending reticular activating system in the rat: A 2-deoxyglucose study. *Brain Research, 344,* 70–88.

Good, T. L., Reys, B. J., Grouws, D. A., & Mulryan, C. M. (1989). Using work-groups in mathematics instruction. *Educational Leadership, 47*(4), 56–62.

Goodwin, C. (1981). *Conversational organization: Interaction between speakers and hearers.* New York, NY: National Academies Press.

Gottfredson, M. R., & Hirschi, T. (1990). *A general theory of crime.* Stanford, CA: Stanford University Press.

Greene, R. W. (2001). *The explosive child.* New York, NY: HarperCollins.

Greene, R. W. (2008). *Lost at school: Why our kids with behavioral challenges are falling through the cracks and how we can help them.* New York, NY: Scribner Books.

Greene, R. W., & Ablon, S. (2005). *Treating explosive kids: The collaborative problem solving approach.* New York, NY: Guilford Press.

Greenspan, S. I. (1979). *Intelligence and adaptation: An integration of psychoanalytic and Piagetian developmental psychology.* New York, NY: International Universities Press.

Greenspan, S. I. (1981). *Psychopathology and adaptation in infancy and early childhood: Principles of clinical diagnosis and preventive intervention.* New York, NY: International Universities Press.

Greenspan, S. I. (1989). Emotional intelligence. In K. Field, B. J. Cohler, & G. Wood (Eds.), *Learning and education: Psychoanalytic perspectives.* Madison, CT: International Universities Press.

Greenspan, S. I. (1993). *Playground and politics: Understanding the emotional life of your school-age child.* Boston, MA: Merloyd Lawrence Books.

Greenspan, S. I. (2009). *Overcoming ADHD: Helping your child become calm, engaged, and focused—Without a pill.* Cambridge, MA: Da Capo Press.

Greenspan, S. I., & Greenspan, N. T. (2010). *The learning tree: Overcoming learning disabilities from the ground up.* Cambridge, MA: Da Capo Press.

Greenspan, S. I., & Shanker, S. (2004). *The first idea: How symbols, language, and intelligence evolved from our primate ancestors to modern humans.* Cambridge, MA: Da Capo Press.

Greenspan, S. I., Wieder, S., & Simons, R. (1998). *The child with special needs: Encouraging intellectual and emotional growth.* New York, NY: Perseus Books.

Greenspan, S., & Wieder, S. (2008). *Engaging autism: Using the floortime approach to help children relate, communicate and think.* Boston, MA: Da Capo Press.

Grossarth-Maticek, R., & Eysenck, H. J. (1995). Self-regulation and mortality from cancer, coronary heart disease, and other causes: A prospective study. *Personality and Individual Differences, 19*(6), 781–795.

Gunnar, M., & Quevedo, K. (2007). The neurobiology of stress and development. *Annual Review of Psychology, 58*, 145–173.

Hart, B., & Risley, T. R. (1995). *Meaningful differences in the everyday experience of young American children.* Baltimore, MD: Paul H. Brookes.

Hirschi, T. (2004). Self-control and crime. In R. F. Baumeister & K. D. Vohs (Eds.), *Handbook of self-regulation: Research, theory, and applications* (pp. 537–552). New York, NY: Guilford Press.

Human Early Learning Partnership. (2010). *Another inconvenient truth: Early childhood vulnerability rises above 30% across 53 school districts.* Retrieved July 16, 2012, from http://earlylearning.ubc.ca/media/uploads/publications/bc_smart_family_policy_report_card_2010_final-_10-09-16_(3).pdf

Human Early Learning Partnership Aboriginal Steering Committee. (2010). *Healthy children, healthy nations: Family policy, cultural vitality, and economic growth.* [Research brief]. Retrieved June 30, 2012, from http://earlylearning.ubc.ca/media/uploads/publications/healthy_children,_healthy_nations_asc_update_2012.pdf

Huttenlocher, P. R. (2002). *Neural plasticity: The effects of environment on the development of the cerebral cortex.* Cambridge, MA: Harvard University Press.

©P

Johnson, D. W., & Johnson, F. P. (2000). *Joining together: Group theory and group skills* (7th ed.). Boston, MA: Allyn and Bacon.

Jones, K., et al. (2005). *Nanny McPhee* [Motion picture]. Universal City, CA: Universal Pictures.

Jones, K., & Day, J. D. (1997). Discrimination of two aspects of cognitive-social intelligence from academic intelligence. *Journal of Educational Psychology, 89*(3), 486–497.

Just Dance (2011, October 3). [Video game]. Kyoto, Japan: Nintendo.

Kagan, J. (1984). *The nature of the child*. New York: NY: Basic Books.

KidsHealth. (n.d.). *About auditory processing disorder*. Retrieved June 2, 2012, from http://kidshealth.org/parent/medical/ears/central_auditory.html

Kim, Y. S., Leventhal, B. L., Koh, Y-J., Fombonne, E., Laska, E., Lim, E-C., Cheon, K-A., Kim, S-J., Kim, Y-K., Lee, H., Song, D-H., Grinker, R. R. (2011). Prevalence of autism spectrum disorders in a total population sample. *AJP in Advance*. Retrieved July 16, 2012, from http://www.autismeurope.org/files/files/new-study-on-autism-prevalence.pdf

King, B. J. (2007). *Evolving God: A provocative view on the origins of religion*. New York, NY: Doubleday.

King, B. J. (2011, September 15). Humans and other animals: a voice from anthropology. Retrieved June 27, 2012, from http://www.npr.org/blogs/13.7/2011/09/15/140461011/humans-and-other-animals-a-voice-from-anthropology

Kirk, S. A., & Kutchins, H. (1992). *The selling of DSM: The rhetoric of science in psychiatry*. Piscataway, NJ: Aldine Transaction.

Kirschner, S., & Tomasello, M. (2010). Joint music making promotes prosocial behaviour in 4-year-old children. *Evolution and Human Behavior, 31*, 354–364.

Knudsen, E. I. (2004). Sensitive periods in the development of the brain and behaviour. *Journal of Cognitive Neuroscience, 16*(8), 1412–1425.

Krugalanski, A. (1978). Endogenous attribution and intrinsic motivation. In D. Greene & M. R. Lepper (Eds.), *The hidden costs of reward*. Hillsdale, NJ: Lawrence Erlbaum.

Lambert, R. G., & McCarthy, C. J. (2006). *Understanding teacher stress in an age of accountability*. Charlotte, NC: Information Age Publishing.

Lawson, C. (2002). The connections between emotions and learning. Retrieved June 15, 2012, from Center for Development and Learning website: http://www.cdl.org/resource-library/articles/connect_emotions.php

Legerstee, M. (2005). *Infants' sense of people: Precursors to a theory of mind*. Cambridge, MA: Cambridge University Press.

Lepper, M. R., Sethi, S., Dialdin, D., & Drake, M. (1997). Intrinsic and extrinsic motivation: A developmental perspective. In S. S. Luthar, J. A. Burack, D. Cicchetti, & J. R. Weisz (Eds.), *Developmental psychology: Perspectives on adjustment, risk, and disorder* (pp. 23–50). New York, NY: Cambridge University Press.

Lepper, M.R., Sagotsky, G., Dafoe, J. L., & Greene, D. (1982). Consequences of superfluous social constraints: Effects on young children's social inferences and subsequent intrinsic interest. *Journal of Personality and Social Psychology, 42*, 51–65.

Lewis, M. D. (2005). Bridging emotion theory and neurobiology through dynamic systems modeling. *Behavioral and Brain Sciences, 28*, 169–194.

Lewis, M. D. (2011). *Memoirs of an addicted brain.* Toronto, ON: Doubleday Canada.

Lewis, M. D., & Todd, R. M. (2007). The self-regulating brain: Cortical-subcortical feedback and the development of intelligent action. *Cognitive Development, 22*(4), 406–430.

Lillas, C., & Turnbull, J. (2009). *Infant/child mental health, early intervention, and relationship-based therapies: A neurorelational framework for interdisciplinary practice.* New York, NY: W. W. Norton.

Lovaas, O. I. (1977). *The autistic child: Language development through behavior modification.* New York, NY: Irvington.

Loveland, K. (2005). Social-emotional impairment and self-recognition in autism spectrum disorders. In J. Nadel & D. Muir (Eds.), *Typical and impaired emotional development* (pp. 365–382). Oxford, UK: Oxford University Press.

Ludwig, T. (2010). *Confessions of a former bully.* New York, NY: Tricycle Press.

Malaguzzi, L. (n.d.). Retrieved June 25, 2012, from http://www.reggiokids.com/about/about_approach.php

McCarthy, J., & Hayes, P. J. (1969). Some philosophical problems from the standpoint of artificial intelligence. In B. Meltzer & D. Michie (Eds.), *Machine intelligence 4* (pp. 463–502). Edinburgh, UK: Edinburgh University Press.

McBride, S. (2008, December). *A cross-Canada review of selected issues in special education.* Victoria, BC: McBride Management.

McCain, M. N., Mustard, J. F., & Shanker, S. G. (2007). *Early years study 2: Putting science into action.* Toronto: The Council for Early Child Development.

McEwen, B. (2002). *The end of stress as we know it.* Washington, DC: National Academies Press.

McEwen, B. (2006). Stress, adaptation, and disease: Allostasis and allostatic load. *Annals of the New York Academy of Sciences, 840*, 33–44.

Mental Health Commission of Canada. (2012). *Changing directions, changing lives: The mental health strategy for Canada.* Retrieved July 16, 2012, from http://www.cpa.ca/docs/file/Practice/strategy-text-en.pdf

Messer, D. J. (1994). *The development of communication: From social interaction to language.* New York, NY: John Wiley & Sons.

Miller, E., & Almon, J. (2009). *Crisis in the kindergarten: Why children need to play in school.* College Park, MD: Alliance for Childhood. Retrieved July 16, 2012, from http://www.eric.ed.gov/PDFS/ED504839.pdf

Molfese, V. J., Molfese, P. J., Molfese, D. L., Rudasill, K. M., Armstrong, N., & Starkey, G. (2010). Executive function skills of 6 to 8 year olds: Brain and behavioral evidence and implications for school achievement. *Contemporary Educational Psychology, 35*(2), 116–125.

Mostrangelo, S. (2010). *Outcomes for families of children with autism spectrum disorder involved in early intervention.* (Unpublished doctoral dissertation). York University, Toronto.

Mundy, P., & Burnette, C. (2005). Joint attention and neurodevelopment models of autism. In F. Vokmar, R. Paul, A. Kim, & D. Cohen (Eds.), *Handbook of autism and pervasive developmental disorders* (3rd ed., pp. 650–681). Hoboken, NJ: Wiley.

Muis, K. R. (2007). The role of epistemic beliefs in self-regulated learning. *Educational Psychologist, 42*(3), 173–190.

Mustard, J. F. (2006). *Early child development and experience-based brain development—The scientific underpinnings of the importance of early child development in a globalized world.* Washington, DC: The Brookings Institute.

Naylor, C., O'Neill, E., & Rojem, K. (2012). Teacher worklife research. BC Teachers' Federation. Retrieved from http://bctf.ca/IssuesInEducation.aspx?id=21453&libID=21443

New Brunswick Department of Education and Early Childhood Development (2008). *New Brunswick Curriculum Framework for Early Learning and Child Care.* Retrieved July 16, 2012, from http://www.gnb.ca/0000/ECHDPE/curriculum-e.asp

Nestle, M. (2007). *Food politics: How the food industry influences nutrition and health* (2nd rev. ed.). Berkeley, CA: University of California Press.

Ninio, A., & Bruner, J. (1978). The achievement and antecedents of labelling. *Journal of Child Language, 5*, 1–15.

Obama, B. (2006, June 16). Northwestern University Commencement Address. Retrieved June 27, 2012, from http://obamaspeeches.com/079-Northwestern-University-Commencement-Address-Obama-Speech.htm

O'Donnell, A. M., & O'Kelly, J. B. (1994). Learning from peers: Beyond the rhetoric of positive results. *Educational Psychology Review, 54*(4), 321–349.

Office of the Surgeon General (US). (2010). *Surgeon General's vision for a healthy and fit nation.* Rockville, MD: Office of the Surgeon General.

Offord, D. R., Boyle, M. H., Fleming, J. E., Munroe Blum, H., & Rae-Grant, N. I. (1989). Ontario child health study: Summary of selected results. *Canadian Journal of Psychiatry, 34*, 483–491.

O'Keefe, M. (2005). Teen dating violence: A review of risk factors and prevention efforts. VAWnet, National Resource Center on Domestic on Violence. Retrieved on July 16, from http://www.unajauladeoro.com/cd/documentos/AR_TeenDatingViolence.pdf

Ontario Ministry of Children and Youth Services. (2006). *A shared responsibility: Ontario's policy framework for child and youth mental health.* Toronto, ON: Queen's Printer.

Ontario Ministry of Children and Youth Services. (2007). *Early learning for every child today.* Retrieved July 16, 2012, from http://www.children.gov.on.ca/htdocs/English/documents/topics/earlychildhood/early_learning_for_every_child_today.pdf

Ontario Ministry of Education. (2008). *Finding common ground: Character development in Ontario schools, K–12.* Toronto, ON: Queen's Printer for Ontario.

Ontario Ministry of Education. (2010). *Health and physical education curriculum for grades 1–8.* Toronto, ON: Ministry of Education.

Ontario Ministry of Education. (2010–11). *The full-day early-learning–Kindergarten program.* Retrieved July 16, 2012, from http://www.edu.gov.on.ca/eng/curriculum/elementary/kindergarten_english_june3.pdf

Oregon State University. (2011, July 18). "Simon says": Preschool-age kids in different countries improve academically using self-regulation game. Retrieved June 26, 2012, from the *ScienceDaily* website: http://www.sciencedaily.com/releases/2011/07/110718151556.htm

Partnership for 21st century skills. (2011). *Partnership for 21st century skills* [Website]. Retrieved July 1, 2012, from http://www.p21.org/index.php

Pascal, C. E. (2009). *Every child, every opportunity: Curriculum and pedagogy for the early learning program.* Retrieved June 6, 2012, from http://ontario.ca/en/initiatives/early_learning/ONT06_023400.html

Perry, N. E., & Rahim, A. (2011). Studying self-regulated learning in classrooms. In B. J. Zimmerman & D. H. Schunk (Eds.), *Handbook of self-regulation of learning and performance* (pp. 122–136). New York, NY: Routledge.

Pfeiffer, B., Henry, A., Miller, S., & Witherell, S. (2008). Effectiveness of Disc 'O' Sit cushions on attention to task in second-grade students with attention difficulties. *American Journal of Occupational Therapy, 62*(3), 274–281.

Pica, R. (2006). Great games for young children: Over 100 games to develop self-confidence, problem-solving skills, and cooperation. Lewisville, NC: Gryphon House.

Pink, D. (2009). *Drive: The surprising truth about what motivates us.* New York, NY: Riverhead Trade.

Plutchik, R. (1980). *Emotion: A psychoevolutionary synthesis.* New York, NY: Harper & Row.

Porges, S. (2011). *The polyvagal theory: Neurophysiological foundations of emotions, attachment, communication, and self-regulation.* New York, NY: Norton.

Preston, S. D., & de Waal, F. B. M. (2002). Empathy: Its ultimate and proximate bases. *Behavioral & Brain Sciences, 25,* 1–72. Retrieved, July 16, 2012, from http://www.emory.edu/LIVING_LINKS/pdf_attachments/Preston_dewaal2002.pdf

Ramachandran, V. S. (2011). The *tell-tale brain: Unlocking the mystery of human nature.* London, UK: William Heinemann.

Rebora, A. (2012, June 8). Study: Teacher PD needs more on emotions. *Education Week Teacher.* Retrieved from http://blogs.edweek.org/teachers/teaching_now/2012/06/study_teacher_pd_needs_more_on_emotions.html?cmp=ENL-EU-NEWS2

Riggs, N. R., Sakuma, K. K., & Pentz, M. A. (2007). Preventing risk for obesity by promoting self-regulation and decision-making skills. *Evaluation Review, 31*(3), 287–310.

Ross, T., & Fontao, M. I. (2008). The relationship of self-regulation and aggression: An empirical test of personality systems interaction theory. *International Journal of Offender Therapy and Comparative Criminology, 52*(5), 554–570.

Safe Schools Manitoba. (2007). Safe schools Manitoba [Website]. Retrieved July 1, 2012, from http://www.safeschoolsmanitoba.ca/Index.htm

Saldanha, C., et al. (2002). *Ice age* [Motion picture]. Beverley Hills, CA: Twentieth Century Fox Home Entertainment.

Scaife, M., & Bruner, J. S. (1975). The capacity for joint visual attention in the infant. *Nature, 253,* 265–266.

Schmeichel, B. J., & Baumeister, R. F. (2004). Self-regulatory strength. In R. F. Baumeister & K. D. Vohs (Eds.), *Handbook of self-regulation* (pp. 84–98). New York, NY: Guilford Press.

Schmidt, N. B., Richey, J. A., & Fitzpatrick, K. K. (2006). Discomfort intolerance: Development of a construct and measure relevant to panic disorder. *Journal of Anxiety Disorders, 20*(3), 263–280.

Seligman, M. E. (1996). *The optimistic child: Proven program to safeguard children from depression and build lifelong resilience.* New York, NY: HarperCollins.

Shanker, S. G. (2001). What children know when they know what a name is. *Current Anthropology, 42*(4), 481–513.

Shanker, S. G., & King, B. J. (2002). The emergence of a new paradigm in ape language research. *Behavioral and Brain Sciences, 25,* 605–656.

Shanker, S. G., & Taylor, T. (2001). The house that Bruner built. In D. Bakhurst & S. Shanker (Eds.), *Language, culture, self: The philosophical psychology of Jerome Bruner* (pp. 50–70). London, UK: Sage Publications.

Shonkoff, J. P., & Phillips, D. A. (2000). *From neurons to neighborhoods: The science of early childhood development.* Washington, DC: National Academies Press.

Soli, S. D., & Devine, V. T. (1976). Behavioral correlates of achievements: A look at high and low achievers. *Journal of Educational Psychology, 68*, 335–341.

Standing Senate Committee on Social Affairs, Science and Technology. (2004). *Time for transformative change: A review of the 2004 health accord.* Ottawa, ON: Senate of Canada.

Statistics Canada. (n.d.). National longitudinal survey of children and youth. Retrieved July 2, 2012, from http://www23.statcan.gc.ca/imdb/p2SV.pl?Function=getSurvey&SDDS=4450&lang=en&db=imdb&adm=8&dis=2

Stieben, J., Lewis, M. D., Granic, I., Zelazo, P. D., Segalowitz, S. J., & Pepler, D. (2007). Neurophysiological mechanisms of emotion regulation for subtypes of externalizing children. *Development & Psychopathology, 19*(2), 455–480.

Stieben, J., Shanker, S. G., & Casenhiser, D. (2012, in prep). Neurophysiological correlates of treatment outcomes in children undergoing a social interaction based treatment for autism spectrum disorders.

Sutton, J., Smith, P. K., & Swettenham, J. (1999). Bullying and "theory of mind": A critique of the "social skills deficit" view of anti-social behaviour. *Social Development, 8*(1), 117–134.

Tantam, D. (2009). *Can the world afford autistic spectrum disorder? Nonverbal communication, asperger syndrome and the interbrain.* London, UK: Jessica Kingsley Publishers.

Taubes, G. (2007). *Good calories, bad calories: Fats, carbs, and the controversial science of diet and health.* New York, NY: Anchor.

Tomkins, S. S. (1963). *Affect imagery consciousness: Vol. 2: The negative affects.* New York, NY: Springer.

Tronick, E. Z. (1989). Emotions and emotional communication in infants. *American Psychologist 44*(2), 112–119.

Trousdale, G., et al. (1991). *Beauty and the beast* [Motion picture]. Burbank, CA: Walt Disney Studios Home Entertainment.

Twenge, J. M. (2006). *Generation me: Why today's young Americans are more confident, assertive, entitled—and more miserable than ever.* New York, NY: Free Press.

Twenge, J. M., & Campbell, W. K. (2009). *The narcissism epidemic: Living in the age of entitlement.* New York, NY: Free Press.

Varela, F. J., Thompson, E., & Rosch, E. (1992). *The embodied mind: Cognitive science and human experience.* Cambridge, MA: MIT Press.

Vygotsky, L. S. (1980). *Mind in society: The development of higher psychological processes* (M. Cole, V. John-Steiner, S. Scribner, & E. Souberman, Eds.). Cambridge, MA: Harvard University Press.

Waddell, C., McEwan, K., Shepherd, C. A., Offord, D. R., & Hua, J. A. (2005). A public health strategy to improve the mental health of Canadian children. *Canadian Journal of Psychiatry, 50*(4), 226–233.

Waddell, C., & Shepherd, C. (2002). *Prevalence of mental disorders in children and youth.* Vancouver, BC: Mental Health Evaluation and Community Consultation Unit, University of British Columbia.

Webb, N. M. (1991). Task-related verbal interaction and mathematics learning in small groups. *Journal for Research on Mathematics Education, 22*(5), 366–389.

Webb, T., Frampton, A., Henderson, E., & Hyman, K. (2009, April). *Teacher wellness in year-round schools: An exploratory study.* Retrieved July 2, 2012, from http://www.sd36.bc.ca/general/news/2009/teacherwellness.pdf

Wenig, M. (1999, March/April). Yoga for kids. In *Yoga Journal.* Retrieved June 15, 2012, from http://www.yogajournal.com/lifestyle/210

Whitebread, D., Bingham, S., Grau, V., Pino Pasternak, D., & Sangster, C. (2007). Development of metacognition and self-regulated learning in young children: The role of collaborative and peer-assisted learning. *Journal of Cognitive Education and Psychology, 3*, 433–455.

Winne, P. H. (2005). A perspective on state-of-the-art research on self-regulated learning. *Instructional Science, 33*, 559–565.

Williams, M. S., & Shellenberger, S. (1996). *"How Does Your Engine Run?"*® *A leader's guide to the Alert Program*® *for self-regulation.* Albuquerque, NM: TherapyWorks, Inc. www.AlertProgram.com

Williams, M. S., & Shellenberger, S. (2001). *Take five! Staying alert at home and school.* Albuquerque, NM: TherapyWorks, Inc. www.AlertProgram.com

Williams, M. S., & Shellenberger, S. (2006). *Test drive: Introducing the Alert Program*® *through song.* Albuquerque, NM: TherapyWorks, Inc. www. AlertProgram.com

Williams, M. S., & Shellenberger, S. (2008). *Keeping on track: Alert Program*® *companion game.* Albuquerque, NM: TherapyWorks, Inc. www.AlertProgram.com

Williams White, S., Koenig, K., & Scahill, L. (2007). Social skills development in children with autism spectrum disorders: A review of the intervention research. *Journal of Autism and Developmental Disorders, 37*(10), 1858–1868.

Willms, J. (2002). The prevalence of vulnerable children. In J. Willms (Ed.), *Vulnerable children: Findings from Canada's National Longitudinal Survey of Children and Youth* (pp. 45–69). Edmonton, AB: The University of Alberta Press.

Wilson, D. S., & Wilson, E. O. (2007, November 3). Survival of the selfless. *New Scientist, 2828*, 42–46.

Woolfolk, A., Winne, P. H., & Perry, N. E. (2009). Teachers, teaching, and educational psychology. In *Educational Psychology* (4th ed., pp. 1–19). Toronto, ON: Pearson Canada.

Wynne, C. D. L. (2004). *Do animals think?* Princeton, NJ: Princeton University Press.

Yerkes, R. M., & Dodson, J. D. (1908). The relation of strength of stimulus to rapidity of habit-formation. *Journal of Comparative Neurology and Psychology, 18*, 459–482.

York Region District School Board. (2010, November). Learning skills and work habits: A guide for elementary and secondary students and their parents/guardians. Retrieved July 1, 2012, from http://www.yrdsb.edu.on.ca/pdfs/w/schools/LearningSkillsandWorkHabitsBrochure.pdf

Zimmerman, B. J. (1990). Self-regulated learning and academic achievement: An overview. *Educational Psychologist, 25*(1), 3–17.

Zimmerman, B. J. (1994). Dimensions of academic self-regulation: A conceptual framework for education. In D. H. Schunk & B. J. Zimmerman (Eds.), *Self-regulation of learning and performance: Issues and educational applications* (pp. 3–21). Hillsdale, NJ: Lawrence Erlbaum Associates.

Zimmerman, B. J., & Campillo, M. (2002). Motivating self-regulated problem solvers. In J. E. Davidson & R. J. Sternberg (Eds.), *The psychology of problem solving* (pp. 233–262). New York, NY: Cambridge University Press.

Zimmerman, B. J., & Schunk, D. H. (Eds.). (2012). *Self-regulated learning and academic achievement: Theory, research, and practice.* New York, NY: Springer.

©P

©P

©P

Risley, Todd, 86
Role models, positive, 117
Roots of Empathy program,
    112–114
Rules in the classroom, 63–64

Salovey, Peter, 32
Scaffolding
    children with special
        needs, 122
    to develop ability to focus,
        52
    helping the frustrated
        child, 145
    and social learning,
        125–127
Scatter Words, 86–87
Schmeichel, B. J., 53
Schmidt, N. B., 84
School choir, 86
Seating in the classroom, 14–15.
    See also Grouping
Second Step program, 97
SEL. *see* Social and emotional
    learning (SEL)
Self-calming behaviours, 126–127
Seligman, Martin, 43
Sensory overload and
    integration, 12–14, 16, 147
Shanker, S. G., 51, 129–130,
    138
Shared gaze, 124
Shellenberger, Sherry, 16–18
Sleep Sheep, 13
Sleeping and waking up, and
    classroom behaviour, 7
SNAP (Stop Now and Plan), 40
SNS. *see* Sympathetic nervous
    system (SNS)
Social and emotional learning
    (SEL), 32, 74

Social domain, xvi–xvii, 73–92
    applications in the
        classroom, 81–92
    collaborative learning,
        80–81
    co-regulation dance, 76
    interactions with other
        domains, 74, 75, 83
    key attributes, 73,
        140–141
    links between regulation,
        self-regulation, and
        co-regulation, 78–80
    promoting self-regulation
        in, 149–150
    social intelligence, 74–76
    strategies for self-regulation
        in, 92
    stress in, 123–124
Social intelligence, xvii, 74–76
Social interactions
    avoiding, 147
    encouraging children with
        special needs, 125–127
    nonverbal and verbal
        signals, 124
Social learning
    children with special
        needs, 123–127
    role of parents, 128–131
    and scaffolding theory,
        125–127
Social skills, 75
    Second Step program, 97
Socio-dramatic play, 49–50
Software, 61–62
Special education. *See also*
    Special needs, children with
    MEHRIT strategy in the
        classroom, 132–133
    programs in Canada, 120

role of self-regulation, 133
and self-regulation,
    120–133
Special needs, children with, 133.
    See also Special education
    social learning, 123–127
    use of MEHRIT program,
        128–133
Steps to Respect program, 96
Stimuli
    modulating intensity of,
        10–11
    sensitivity to, 84, 125–127
Stop Now and Plan. *see* SNAP
    (Stop Now and Plan)
Strategies snapshots
    encouraging emotion
        regulation, 43–44
    enhancing students' ability
        to pay attention, 71–72
    enhancing the classroom
        environment, 20–21
    guiding children to self-
        and co-regulate, 118
    promoting social self-
        regulation, 92
Stress. *See also* Human nervous
    system
    and mental health, 142
    in parents of children with
        autism, 131
    in prosocial domain,
        101–102, 123–124
    in social domain, 123–124
Sympathetic nervous system
    (SNS), 2–3, 83
    definition, 2

Taylor, T., 51
Teachers
    burnout among, 151

15: (photo) Courtesy of Louise Kiner; **17:** (figure) Courtesy of Mary Sue Williams and Sherry Shellenberger. Adapted from materials in the book, *"How Does Your Engine Run?"*® *A Leader's Guide to the Alert Program*® *for Self-Regulation* by Mary Sue Williams and Sherry Shellenberger (1996). Albuquerque, NM: TherapyWorks, Inc. www.AlertProgram.com; **26:** (photo) Chartres Cathedral, Chartres, France/The Bridgeman Art Library; **39:** (figure) Courtesy of Markus Drews; **40:** (box) Child Development Institute, Toronto, CANADA www.stopnowandplan.com; **52:** (figure) The Temporal Dynamics Model of Emotional Memory Processing: A Synthesis on the Neurobiological Basis of Stress-Induced Amnesia, Flashbulb and Traumatic Memories, and the Yerkes-Dodson Law http://www.ncbi.nlm.nih.gov/pmc/articles/PMC1906714/?tool=pubmed; **63:** (figure) From "Motivating Self-Regulated Problem Solvers" by B. J. Zimmerman & M. Campillo (2003), pp. 233–262. In J. E. Davidson & R. J. Sternberg (Eds.), *The Psychology of Problem Solving*. New York: Cambridge University Press. Copyright by Cambridge University Press.